MARK COLES

LEVEL UP

THE FITNESS PROFESSIONAL'S ROAD MAP TO ACHIEVING EXCELLENCE

RETHINK PRESS

First published in Great Britain in 2020
by Rethink Press (www.rethinkpress.com)

© Copyright Mark Coles

Cover design concept: Marsha Coles

Interior image of human body © Shutterstock | Digital Storm

Disclaimer: The use of any information in this book, including any medical, diet and nutritional information is solely at the reader's own risk. The author and the publisher advise the reader to seek medical advice before undertaking any specific medical, diet or nutrition plans.

Contents

Foreword

Walking into a swanky upscale coffee shop in February 2013, I glanced around and spotted the only guy in the place with a neck that resembled a prized Belgian blue bull. I knew I had the right guy.

I had been hired for a consult in Tampa, Florida, after a referral from a friend and was meeting Mark Coles for the first time.

Unsure of the direction of the impending conversation, I was welcomed by a strong handshake from a hand the size of a grizzly bear's, and a confident smile that could only be delivered by someone who had earned his place at the table of life.

Within minutes of meeting Mark, it became apparent that his knowledge was decades beyond any other personal trainer I had ever met, and his business and leadership acumen reflected years of successful time in the trenches of building and growing a real business.

Mark and I spent hours talking, sharing, and getting to know each other, and have since gone on to become life-long friends. We spent a month training together in Tampa, travelled throughout California, attended business events, recorded educational podcasts, and consumed copious numbers of protein-dense meals. Yet, every single time I have the privilege of seeing or speaking with Mark, he has grown as a man, up-levelled his life, and lives in 100% alignment with the incredibly high standard I have always known him for maintaining in all aspects of his life: personally, professionally and physically.

When Mark called to ask me to write the foreword for his book, not only was I honoured, but truly excited for what I knew he was about to reveal to the world.

You see, regardless of our friendship, Mark is one of the few people in the world that should actually be writing books. In 2020, everyone is jumping on the book writing bandwagon. It's the cool thing to do.

Everyone wants to be a coach, or a mentor, or a business guru, but not many of them have put in the time to do their homework, build an actual business, or have any unique thought that will provide something of value for its readers.

Like you, I place a huge value on every minute of my life. I've started and stopped a lot of books that just didn't offer anything more than regurgitated fluff. If I'm going to read a book, take a course or listen to someone speak, I have to be 100% sure it's worth investing my time and money in.

I have already read this book twice. I took fourteen pages of notes and spent hours working deeply on five action items that Mark guides us through in the pages of *Level Up*.

Take out a pen, a notepad and pay attention. Although it's easy to read, this is not the type of book you should breeze through.

When Mark speaks, writes, or teaches, don't just listen, DO what he says.

If you want to succeed in the fitness industry and create a life you love, adopting Mark's framework around the 3-Ps should be a must.

Until very recently, creating a business that flourishes as a personal trainer or coach was uncertain and often painful. You had to go through it yourself to understand what was really necessary and this can take years. Ten plus years.

Luckily for you, the 'information age' allows us all to have access to the wisdom of the leaders in society like never before. We can hack their brains, download their systems, and learn from their immense wisdom.

Mark Coles is a leader in the fitness industry.

The quote, 'You don't know what you don't know' is a quote that Mark and I have discussed at length as we support each other's ongoing personal development and keep ourselves accountable for always seeking to Level Up.

This book provides clarity in areas that you don't even know you don't know.

The stories of Mark's experiences and those of his clients paint the perfect picture to convey his point and empower trainers with a thought process and skillset to learn what to listen for, ask better questions, and make quick changes to their own lives, and in getting rapid results for clients.

Every single section of this book is power-packed with wisdom to Level Up your life.

While some people will sell you the false truth of a big social media following being the key to increased credibility and making more money, they fail to recognise the mirage of social media is that many people with hundreds of thousands of followers often aren't making money, while people with just a few hundred can be making millions each year, and living a life of freedom that serves them, rather than enslaves them.

The fact that you're here reading this now, tells me you're not one to sit around and hope things will one day land in your lap. You're someone who is committed to taking action. Kudos to you, as that is step one. This book will act as your guide: use it as a road map to achieve success in your personal, physical and professional life.

Ben Pakulski
IFBB Pro, High Performance Coach and Speaker

Introduction

A re you a fitness coach who wants more for yourself and for your career? Do you think you're working hard and doing all the right things, only to find you're not progressing at the rate that you expected? Are you hoping that all the hard work you're putting in will magically pay off sometime soon?

Wouldn't it be wonderful to know a better way and to stop the guessing?

I know how you feel. I felt that way, too, until I found a smarter way to achieve excellence through hard work and a lot of self-improvement. I've been in the fitness industry for nineteen years, and I know only too well the hurdles that every fitness professional will run into.

We should never see ourselves as complete; we should always be works in progress. But I have reached a stage in my career where I know that my experiences and lessons need to be shared because they can be of value to you.

I want to equip you with as many tools as possible so that you are able to navigate the fitness industry and achieve your own level of success. Throughout your career, there will inevitably be roadblocks – trust me, I've had to work my way through many. Whenever you hit one, I want you to be able to pick up this book, go to a relevant section and find something that will help you along your way.

Level Up is about progress; it's not about status or a final destination. It's about appreciating that you won't become the person you want to be or have the business and the life that you want, without some change. For every big step that you want to take, you are going to have to Level Up in some way. As you read this book, I want you to be able to identify key areas where you can Level Up.

I've always said to myself, 'If I can just be one level better than where I am right now, I'll be moving forward and making progress.' It's easy to become overwhelmed with big goals, which is why it's so important to have a Level Up mindset.

I want *Level Up* to act like a mentor for you, guiding you through key challenges that I know you're going to run into, answering questions that I know you're going to ask, and providing insight from someone who has been where you are heading.

I want you to know that where I am today is the result of constant questioning, setting specific goals and challenges for myself, and doing everything in my power to meet them. I created every step of my journey, and I want you to know that you can create your own version of success, too. I don't expect you to copy every step of my journey; I want you to follow your own path.

What I am going to provide you with is a road map. One that I have adjusted over the years. I've mentored hundreds of personal trainers and fitness professionals using the process that I'm going to set out in the sections that follow.

The Level Up road map

The Level Up road map is a 360-degree approach to yourself, your clients and your business. The 360 degrees of excellence questions in this book have kept me inspired, motivated and constantly levelling up. The Level Up road map is organised into three parts: personal, physical and professional.

The Personal – Be More! road map will help you break through personal limitations and strive for excellence.

The Physical – Learn More! road map will help you improve your coaching skills, knowledge, results and reputation in the fitness industry.

The Professional – Do More! road map will increase your business acumen, your levels of professionalism, and your understanding of marketing, money and sales.

I wanted to write *Level Up* to give back to an industry that has helped me so much. I want to share many of my lessons and experiences and give you the same opportunity to have a fulfilling, successful and happy career.

I've had the honour of learning from some great mentors and coaches over my long career. One stands out: the late Charles Poliquin, who I first visited in Santander, Spain, in 2008. It was clear right from the start that Charles had high standards for everything that he did, and I came back from Spain with an unbelievable fire in my belly. I had witnessed a level of coaching, knowledge and professionalism that inspired me and was fully aligned with what I wanted to be known for.

I wasn't delusional about my own position; I knew that I had a long road ahead of me. I just felt that I had seen a standard that I could set as a benchmark for my future. When I got back home, I sat in the reception of the gym with a pad full of notes. I'd been on one hell of a journey in Spain. I had discovered personal and professional development, and I was already noticing a huge shift in how I was thinking and feeling about my life, my business and the direction that I wanted to go in.

My newfound knowledge had given me a big lift in confidence, which was having a positive impact on my results with my clients. I folded over to a new page in my note pad and wrote some more. I acknowledged that personal development was going to play a big part in my progression in the fitness industry. I wrote that I wanted to develop my reputation and be known for my results, and that I wanted to learn more about developing my business.

I had started to piece it all together. If I wanted to get somewhere with my business and with my life, I was going to have to take control of them. I was going to have to work out exactly what I wanted every part of my business and my life to look like, and I was going to have to put everything in place to make it happen.

I had moved from being someone who battled with low self-confidence and struggled to learn to being someone who was excited about all of the challenges that lay ahead.

360 degrees of excellence

The Success Principles by Jack Canfield,[1] about how to get from where you are now to where you want to be, had a big impact on me. I used a lot of what I learned in that book as a reference and created a set of questions that would help me to Level Up:

1. Am I growing as a person?
2. Am I developing a better reputation?
3. Are my results where I want them to be?
4. Is my business growing?

At the end of each day, run through the four simple questions above. Make notes, identify the gaps, resolve to find solutions and take action. This will ensure you always working towards 360 degrees of excellence.

As I asked myself each of these questions, I would see if there was something in Canfield's book that would help me to answer it. *When I reached an answer, whatever it was, I would go away and take action on it.* There were many times when I tried something and it didn't work for me, or it just didn't feel right, but it didn't matter; I always wanted to see if the things that I was learning could help me.

---

1   J Canfield, *The Success Principles: How to get from where you are to where you want to be* (Harper Collins, 2015)

I had started to develop a nice framework for myself. Every time I felt a little stuck, I would run through the same questions. If something wasn't aligned, I would go in search of the answer. It might have meant travelling to attend a course, reaching out to someone for advice or reading a book.

Slowly but surely, my reputation was increasing. I could see myself growing as a person, my coaching results were getting so much better, and my business was developing.

When I started mentoring personal trainers, I took each of the questions and broke them down further. I wrote down all of the strategies that I had focused on to progress myself in each area of my business and my life, and I organised them into three parts:

1. I had worked on my mindset every step of the way (Personal)

2. I had committed a great deal of time to learning about the body and how that transferred into the results that I achieved with my clients (Physical)

3. I had focused on the development of my business knowledge and learning how to apply it to see consistent business growth (Professional)

The Level Up road map that I'm going to share with you consists of these three parts – Personal, Physical and Professional.

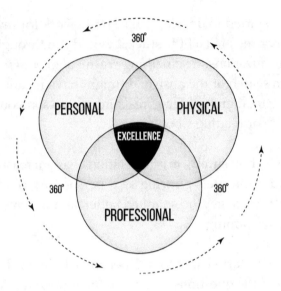

Personal

I have a saying that I share with everyone that I work with: 'The person you are today isn't going to be the same person who will achieve your life and business vision.' What I mean by this is that *for you to progress towards your life and business goals, you are going to have to grow alongside them.* As you progress, it's likely that you'll run into personal limitations such as low self-confidence, doubt, frustration and fear. You will need to know what they mean and how to deal with them when they show up. You'll need to learn to apply discipline, focus and effort for every level that you want to climb. You'll need to develop personal standards that match the goals you have for yourself.

When I work with any coach who is looking to progress their career, I always start with the personal aspects. I remember reading once that professional problems are often personal problems, and after years of mentoring coaches I can confirm that this is true. A winning mindset is something that has to be created and continuously worked at, so in this part of the book I'll be sharing strategies that will help you to understand obstacles as they arise, while also helping you to create a powerful and unstoppable mindset.

Physical

If you've followed my work, you'll know that I've taken the development of my body seriously throughout my entire career. I see each of our bodies as a gift; it's the most incredible canvas that we have the privilege of working on and learning from every day. As you will also read in the Personal sections of this book, I believe that we should work to become masters of ourselves as well as masters of our craft.

I come across so many coaches who aren't committing themselves anywhere near enough to their physical progression. How can you expect to help people get the best out of themselves if you're not committed to getting the best out of yourself?

The physical aspect of my mentoring road map is all about understanding and education. How committed are you to the development and understanding of your own body, and how does that carry over to the results you want to achieve with your clients? Are there areas that you could be focusing on that would improve your knowledge of your clients and help you to achieve higher-quality results? Are there areas that you could be focusing on that would help you develop your reputation and take your career in the direction that you envision?

All too often, coaches work alone and don't have a reference of where they should be or what's required of them if they want to get to the next level. In this part of the book, I'm going to provide you with some challenging questions so you can see if you're where you should be. I'm going to share strategies with you that will help you to Level Up, which will dramatically impact your progression, your reputation, your results and the development of your business.

Professional

I've had the privilege, from an early age, of watching my father pursue his business ambitions, and I've also worked alongside him. His drive, passion and commitment had a huge impact in creating the businessperson that I am today. I will be forever grateful for his constant guidance and support.

From the moment I started in the fitness industry, I resolved to prove to my dad that I could create a business. I wasn't just going to train people; I was going to create a career and reputation for myself. I didn't know how; I just knew that I was going to do it. Hearing Charles Poliquin talk about business at his seminar in Spain confirmed that business development was going to be very important for me. Over the years, I've not only studied a great deal about business, I've also been (and continue to be) mentored by some incredibly successful people. Each of them shared years of wisdom that I would have never picked up from courses or books.

As I started to mentor more and more coaches, it became clear that business was an area of knowledge that was lacking for so many of them. I always say, if you want to grow a business you need to know business. Business isn't taught enough to fitness professionals; this could be why you're struggling to make progress.

In this part of the book, I am going to teach you how to develop the mindset of a business owner. I'm going to share strategies that will help you to deliver a more professional service to your clients. I'm also going to teach you the most important areas to focus on to support the growth of your fitness business: results, reputation and revenue.

Mark Coles' ten lessons for fitness professionals

Before we get started, I want to share some valuable lessons that I picked up from my early years:

1. Don't hold onto the old version of you. Be grateful for who you were, but also acknowledge that a new version of you is the one who will take you forward. You will go through plenty of versions of you as you progress through your life.

2. People will come and go in your life, and you have to be OK with that. The people who matter the most will always support your growth. The people who have an issue with what you're trying to achieve don't matter.

3. When you want to pursue a dream, you will face lonely times. In order to achieve something that is truly important to you, you will have to make some sacrifices along the way.

4. Just be you. I spent a lot of my childhood trying to be someone else. I found true happiness when I started to be true to myself.

5. Listen intently to successful people. If you're ever in the presence of successful people, ask questions and listen to their advice. They are full of little gems that will transform the way that you think about business and life.

6. Follow your passion, and don't stop until you find it. I made an early mistake of following what I thought I should do. Your passion is where you are truly the most inspired and energised. Find yours!

7. Don't limit your learning to one place. Throughout my early days, I travelled the world in search of the right people who had the knowledge that I needed. Be prepared to travel to develop yourself and your business.

8. Don't be afraid to make a mistake. I learned more from my mistakes than I did from my successes. Whenever I made a mistake, I would look for the lesson that I could learn from it.

9. Be patient. I know you want to achieve big things in your career, but you can't build a successful business without solid foundations, and foundations take time to build.

10. Don't rush to be something that you're not. You will develop your expertise over time but be grateful for what you know now and serve the audience that is aligned with your current knowledge, experience and skillset.

It's now time to start your Level Up journey. I hope you're ready.

PART ONE
Personal – Be More!

For most of my career, personal development has played a huge part in my life. I had the great fortune to meet Jane – a client who helped me as much as I helped her – early in my career, when I was only twenty-four years old. While I trained her, she introduced me to the concept of personal growth. Conversations with Jane were so inspiring, she was always positive, and she followed every single piece of advice I gave her. I can't recall a day where Jane turned up in a bad mood or showed any signs of being demotivated.

They say people come into your life at the right time.

While my personal development has been a challenging journey, I can honestly say that without it I would not be the man that I am today, nor would I have achieved the things that I have. I incorporated everything that you're about to read into the personal training sessions that I have delivered to my clients over the years, and I have carried it over into the mentoring that I do with fitness professionals all over the world.

This may be your first introduction to personal growth, so let me explain what it is. It is a commitment that you make to constant growth and taking full responsibility for the direction that you want your life to go in. It's learning habits that help you to keep progressing while also remaining in control of your thoughts, behaviour and actions. I call my approach 360 degrees of excellence because I like to refer to personal development as the pursuit of excellence, and there is no finish line when you are in the pursuit of excellence.

Many people remain unaware that their daily behaviours, thoughts, beliefs and actions are shaping a life that is completely opposite to what they truly want. In fact, a lot of people haven't even identified what they want out of their lives. The easiest way to describe someone like this is 'out of control'. Maybe you feel out of control now. If so, know that personal development is all about taking full control of your life.

PIT STOP

When you think of someone who is making constant progress with their business and their life, what attributes would you associate with them? Here are a few that will definitely be on the list: confident, focused, clear, passionate, driven, decisive, goal orientated, happy.

Now think of someone who is struggling to make progress. What attributes would you associate with them? They may include low in self-confidence, frustrated, self-doubting, confused, unhappy, easily distracted, comparing themselves to others.

Now take a moment to look at both lists. Which one can you relate to at this stage in your life?

In my early years, I struggled with low self-confidence, I doubted myself and I was very unhappy. A lot of this stemmed from not achieving a great deal at school, which left me questioning my intelligence and ability. I managed to scrape through my GCSEs and A levels. The only thing that kept me focused at school was my love of sport. It was never a surprise to my parents that my grades were a lot better in the rugby season!

I realised that if I wanted to achieve all that I wanted to, I had to address the issues first. The good news is, it's possible to change, to work on yourself, and to develop new habits.

Many people think that they're dealt a certain hand in life – you are the way that you are. This is so far from the truth. You are simply a new level of knowledge and action away from living the life that you truly want.

Now, you might be thinking, 'Well, I don't have any so-called issues, so this doesn't apply to me.' Here's the thing: personal growth isn't specifically for people who are struggling; it's also for people who might be doing well but want to do even better. *If you're someone who values growth and development, you will know that we should always be works in progress.*

Limitations

The first area that I'm going to discuss is limitations. These are the areas that are likely to be holding you back at the moment. To make any level of progress, awareness of your limitations in your life or business is essential.

When it comes to personal growth, many people choose to hold on to their limitations. Rather than choosing to move on from them and pushing forward, they choose to fall back into them like a kind of safety net. Every time you choose to fall back, you are feeding your limitations. It's easy to use your limitations as an excuse for your lack of progress. People will often say that they struggle with X and this is the reason why they're not where they want to be.

A limitation is essentially something that we think we can't do, a restriction that we have in place. It might look something like, 'I'm scared of something', 'I don't think I can do something', 'I'm not good enough' or 'I just don't think it's possible'. You might also know limitations as self-doubt, fear and lack of self-confidence. Remember at the beginning of the book I talked about my own limitations and how I left school doubting that I would amount to anything. If that limitation was still in place today, there is no way I would have achieved the things that I have.

Limitations are often a result of events that have happened in your life. I didn't do well in my studies at school, so as a result I didn't think I would ever be smart enough to grow my reputation and my business in the fitness industry. I had a choice between leaving that limitation where it was, and allowing it to shape the rest of my life, or accepting that at school I might not have learned a great deal but knowing that this doesn't stop me from learning what I missed out on now. I chose the latter and dedicated myself to education and bettering myself.

I have a strong belief that all limitations or obstacles can be overcome, and in the majority of cases they can be overcome by focusing on the future as opposed to the past. However, there are cases where you will need to take time to address your relationship with specific events from your past. My advice is to use the strategies that I share with you in this book first. If you feel like you can't break through your limitations and that the strategies aren't helping you, then seek professional advice.

PIT STOP

Take some time to think about your own limitations. Do you have any? If you sit back and think about where you want to get to in your life and with your business, is there anything that you feel is holding you back?

Now let me ask you: if you had some strategies to help you progress away from your current feelings, would you implement them? I'd like to think that your answer is 'yes'.

At this stage, I want to give you another way of looking at limitations. It's a strategy that I learned a long time ago that helped me to progress immensely, and I now teach it to the many fitness professionals that I mentor. It involves learning how to reframe the language that you use when you speak to yourself.

Carol Dweck, in her book *Mindset*, talks about the fixed mindset versus the growth mindset. The fixed mindset is locked into stagnation and limitations. The growth mindset sees explanations and opportunity behind every situation.[2]

Imagine parking your car on double yellow lines and receiving a parking ticket on your return. Most people blame the parking attendant for the fact that

---

2   C Dweck, *Mindset: How you can fufil your potential* (Robinson, 2012)

they've now got a ticket. Now imagine if you change the language that you use and look at the situation differently. You are choosing to park in a space that is clearly marked as 'no parking' (by the double yellow lines). So, as you leave your car you say to yourself, 'I fully appreciate that I may receive a ticket, as I understand that I shouldn't be parking here.' You have taken immediate responsibility for the situation, and in doing so you have a completely different perspective on the situation when you return to your car.

Understanding this principle changed my mindset forever. The reason I didn't do well at school had nothing to do with the school itself or the lack of support from the teachers; it was down to me not applying myself. The education was there for me – I chose not to follow it.

I will never forget one special conversation I had with Jane during a training session. We were talking about achievement and she said, 'Everyone has the opportunity to have whatever they want in life.' I immediately resisted and said that was absolute rubbish. I said, 'You are dealt a hand in life, you get what you get.' She disagreed and told me that anyone can change: 'Yes, of course we develop through life with specific values and beliefs, but we can change them if we don't like them.'

This was the conversation that marked the start of the biggest journey of my life. I went home that night and went over and over Jane's statement. Is it really possible to have whatever you want in life?

I later asked her, 'Jane, how does someone change if they want to be something, but they don't think it's possible?' She said, 'It's all about mindset. It's being able to shift from a limited level of thinking to a limitless level of thinking.'

I had said to myself early in my career that I wasn't clever enough to build a business and a reputation; after talking to Jane, I changed the language that I used when thinking about myself. It became, 'When I learn what I don't yet know, I will be able to build a successful business and grow my reputation.' This filled me with excitement, because I realised for the first time in my life that my future was in my hands.

PIT STOP

Try to reframe some of the language that you're using about yourself. Are you only in your current situation or thinking that you have limitations because you haven't learned how to progress forward? Are you only stuck where you are right now because you haven't taken the necessary action?

Where could you be in the next six months if you layered on a new level of knowledge, and if you fully committed yourself to progress?

Understand that you're either choosing to let your limitations hold you back or you're going to use them to help propel yourself forward. As this book is all about levelling up, let's focus on the latter.

A great mentor of mine once advised me to focus so hard on my future that my past drifts into insignificance. I love this because I used to let my past define me; I used to allow it to hold me back. But as soon as I started to focus on where I wanted to go and what I needed to do to get there, any self-doubt or limitations that I had quickly started to fade away.

I hope you can now see that self-doubt and limitations are all messages. You wouldn't be feeling this way about yourself if you weren't trying to excel in certain areas of your life. You're simply looking at something that you want and thinking that you can't have it before you've even looked at the possibilities that are in front of you. People who aren't trying to progress don't get any feelings of doubt because they're not making any effort to better themselves. They have no reason to doubt themselves. Self-doubt and the feelings of limitation are good things; use them to your advantage.

Is everything holding you back going to disappear overnight? No. Can you put in the work to move away from where you are right now? Yes, 100%.

Creating a clear vision

One of the best ways to start your personal growth is to set a crystal-clear vision for your future. As one of my mentors said to me, you have to focus all of your efforts on your future. If you don't have an idea of what you want that to look like, you don't have anything to work towards.

Your vision is all about your destination. Where do you want to be in the next six months, and in one, three, and five years? What do you want your business and life to look like? Understand that every action that you take today is contributing to your ultimate destination. If you're not actioning every day with clear intention, you have no control of your destination.

Your vision will always be subject to change as you navigate through your life, but you need an inspiring vision that will feed your motivation and drive every day. When I speak to fitness professionals who lack motivation, often I see that they haven't got a clear vision for their life or for their business.

PIT STOP

Your vision isn't something that you should be able to jot down as you're reading through this book; it's something that you should take time over. I advise you to take yourself somewhere quiet, allow yourself a good few hours and let your brain dump ideas onto a piece of paper. Start with your five-year vision; what do you want your life to look like in five years' time? What have you achieved, what are you known for, where are you living, how much are you earning, how do you feel? Then, do the same for three years, one year and six months. When you have competed this task, you should have four sections completed.

To make this process even more powerful, take your five-year vision and write it out as a letter to yourself from the future, as if it has already happened.

Here is an example of a letter to myself:

I am living in Scotland with my wife and two children. We live in a four-bedroom house that has a drive for our two cars, and we have a large garden out the back where my children can play. I have my own personal training studio and I have three coaches working for me. We are very well known for the work that we do with weight loss and helping people to find happiness within themselves and their health. I am delivering twenty hours a week of personal training because this is my passion, and the rest of my time is spent running the studio alongside my full-time studio administrator. I also run our twelve-week online weight-loss challenge, where we are helping over fifty people every twelve weeks from all over the world.

My family and I go on two holidays every year, and I am able to save enough income to put some into trust for my children's education as they grow up. We are very happy as a family, I have fantastic team working with me in the business, and I have time to enjoy my social life with my friends.

While this is just an example, can you feel how powerful this type of letter would be to someone who is struggling with direction and purpose. From here, you are able to work your way backwards, performing a process that I call 'reverse engineering'. What has to happen in the next six months to one year that will enable you to live this kind of life in five years' time? Again, this process does take time, but when you have finished you will have goals, targets and a clear vision of where you will end up if you take action every day.

I will never forget one day in my second year as a personal trainer. I was sitting in the café area of LA Fitness in my hometown of Newark. I was doing over thirty-five sessions of personal training each week, and I loved all of my clients and the results that they were achieving, but it just started to feel like there wasn't any real direction. The issue I was facing was that I had lost a part of my vision. I was waking up every day to coach my clients, but I had lost sight of what I was working towards.

It was at that moment that my vision was born. I sat there for what felt like ages, until I decided that I did not only want to be known in my gym; I wanted everyone in my county, and eventually the whole country, to know about me. I wanted people everywhere to know me for the quality and consistency of my results. I remember saying to myself that I would be one of the best-known coaches in the country. To achieve this, I was going to have to Level Up big time. I was going to have to achieve better results, and I was also going to have to start sharing what I knew. So, I spent the next twenty-four hours creating a road map of how this was going to happen.

The morning after this revelation, I woke up determined to build my reputation and introduce more people to my work and the knowledge that I was developing. I knew it was going to be a long road – and, if I'm honest, I didn't know how I was going to get there – but the vision was crystal clear.

Jane gave me a book called *The Secret* by Rhonda Byrne.[3] It changed my way of thinking dramatically. The subject of the book is the law of attraction, and it takes you on a journey where you look deeply into how you process your thoughts, behaviours and actions. If you channel them in the right way, you are able to attract everything that you ever want into your world. The first step is deeply thinking about what you want, and the second step is acting every day in accordance with the things that you want the most. Think about that for a second: are your daily actions in line with what you say you want?

---

3   R Byrne, *The Secret* (Simon & Schuster, 2006)

For many fitness professionals, there is a lot of talk about goals but very little action. Think about where you could be right now if you went about every single day focused and intent on where you want to get to.

This is what I started to do. I became relentless; I was so focused on growing my reputation that I would question every single task that I was doing every day. I used to say to myself, 'Is what I'm doing complementing the direction that I want my life to go in or complicating it?' To this day, this is one of the most powerful things that I teach fitness professionals. Every day must have purpose, every task must have an outcome, and that outcome must always be linked to your vision.

As I progressed through my journey in the fitness industry and started to mentor more fitness professionals, I began to realise that a clear vision wasn't something that came naturally to everyone. I would ask coaches to take themselves away and come back to me with their vision planned out, and they would come back and say that they were really struggling.

To try to get to the bottom of this problem, I started by questioning myself more. Why had I been able to create my vision so effortlessly? All that kept coming back to me was that I knew I was doing what I truly loved, and I wanted to help as many people as I could.

So, I started to ask the coaches that I was working with why they were doing what they were doing. It was clear to me that many were operating their businesses and lives with very little thought. I needed to find a way of helping each of them to create their vision and clarify the direction that they wanted their life and their business to go in.

Living your life according to your values

It was around this time that I went to London to listen to Dr John Demartini speak. I had first been introduced to his work in *The Secret*.

It took one evening in the company of this man for me to understand so much about what had got me to this point in my life.

Dr Demartini spoke about the concept of values – each person's ability to truly determine what is important to them in their life. To fully appreciate the magnificence of his work, I am going to suggest that you either read his book *The Values Factor* or that you attend his Breakthrough Experience event.

Most people cannot determine where they want to get to (vision) simply because they haven't identified what they want to get out of life and what they want to achieve. When you have been able to identify your values, you will have a new sense of purpose and meaning, you will be inspired, and you will also be able to create a crystal-clear vision. Dr Demartini's work not only helped me to realign my own values and gain a deeper level of clarity about the direction that I want my own life to go in; it also gave me a road map that I was able to use to help coaches excel in their lives.

Again, this is a process that you need to take time over; don't expect to start now and have it all done in half an hour. By the time you have gone through the values process, you will have found a new level of inspiration and motivation. You will start waking up every day tingling with excitement to drive your life and business forward.

Many people set their goals and vision based on what other people are doing. They think that because one person has chosen a certain path it's right for them to follow the same one. If you do this, you'll find that years down the line you're not fulfilled, you're not happy, and you certainly won't have made anywhere near the level of progress that you would have expected. The journey that you map out (vision) should be for you, in line with everything that you truly want out of life, and in line with everything that you are truly inspired by. These are the things you're about to discover about yourself.

Dr Demartini poses thirteen questions to help you identify what you value most in your life. I have shared seven of the main ones with you below, as I want you to invest in Dr Demartini's book to take your understanding of values to the next level and learn directly from his work.[4]

Read the questions below and provide three answers to each question.

1. What do you spend most of your time doing?

2. What do you spend most of your money on?

3. What areas of your life do you have the most discipline and focus in?

4. What occupies most of your thoughts throughout each day?

5. What subject(s) would you most enjoy talking about socially?

6. What inspires you the most?

7. What subjects do you love to learn the most about?

Once you have your answers written down, write down which answer appears the most as your number one answer. Repeat for your number-two and number-three answers. You'll begin to see some similarities among your answers. The answer that has appeared as number one the most is where you are

---

4 J Demartini, *The Values Factor: The secret to creating an inspired and fulfilling life* (Berkley Books, 2013)

going to be the most inspired and motivated; this will be followed by your second and third choices.

Throughout the first fourteen years of my career, the areas that I valued the most were my training, my clients/business, and developing my education. If I was doing anything that was linked to any of my highest values, I was seriously motivated and inspired. Looking back to my vision, I didn't realise it at the time, but I was fixated on learning more and building my reputation. It was deeply rooted in me, and by going through this process I just brought it to the surface.

Within the last four years, my values have changed dramatically; they are now my wife and our life, business development and helping fitness professionals, and my own training. If I am doing anything that is linked to these values, I am truly the most inspired and motivated.

If you've been feeling unmotivated and uninspired, this process is going to be a complete game changer for you. After you have been through it and identified your highest values, go back to your vision and see if it's easier to map out. You might have set out your vision thinking that you knew what you wanted out of life and for your business, but your realigned values might have challenged those ideas.

Remember that your journey through life will be forever changing. As you grow and progress in your career, your values will change, which will have an impact on your vision. For example, you might achieve more than you thought you would, giving you a surge in confidence. With that comes a clearer vision for what else you could achieve. This is why it's important for you to take time for yourself every six months and review your vision and values.

Having a clear vision and inspiring values doesn't mean that it's job done; it's only the start. To ensure that you're equipped for the journey towards your vision, I believe that you need a toolbox of powerful attributes – a set of characteristics which I call your 'excellence attributes' that support your vision.

Excellence attributes

'Excellence' is an important word, and that's because I don't see excellence as being absolute. The 'ence' part means that excellence doesn't have a finish line. I believe we should always be evolving and in pursuit of improvements across all areas of our lives, and that's what I mean by 360 degrees of excellence.

This falls perfectly in line with the idea of Level Up, as I don't see there being a level that defines you as 'finished'. If you're at the start of your career, then you are going to make a great deal of progress if you step up one level. If you've been in the industry a long time, there is always another level that you can move up towards.

Excellence attributes:

1. Internally driven

2. Competitive, but on your own terms

3. Confident in your own abilities

4. Clear thinker

5. Action taker

6. Analytical

7. Growth minded

8. Optimistic

9. Passionate

I'll explain each of these attributes in greater detail and give you some areas in which you can take action immediately.

Internally driven

The 'internally driven' attribute links so well with values and vision. All too often people will ask me why they struggle with drive and motivation. The reason is because they're not linking their daily tasks to their values and vision. The linking process allows you to look at any task that you have to perform and immediately see its value. Let me give you an example: You feel like you're not driven or motivated to speak to people on the gym floor. You know it's something that you need to do, but every time you have a break you do anything to avoid being on the gym floor. Then, you take a step back and look at your values; you remind yourself that one of your highest values is helping people to reach their fitness and health goals. You now link speaking to people on the gym floor to helping people. If you don't spend time speaking to people, how are you ever going to help them to reach their health and fitness goals? In fact, sitting in the café area and avoiding speaking to people is taking you further and further away from living your highest value.

I'll share one more: You sit down and procrastinate over writing content for your social media posts. It doesn't matter how long you look at the computer, you can't seem to make any progress. Then you take a step back and look at your values, and one of your highest ones is developing your reputation. If you don't commit to time creating content, you'll never reach enough people to grow your reputation. That simple linking process is enough to take you back to your computer screen and back to creating content.

Try linking for yourself. After a short period of time, you'll be so good at linking that you'll have endless drive and motivation. Initially, you'll need your values written down so that you can reference them – in fact, I advise you to have them written on a whiteboard at home so you can see them every morning before you start your day. You can't grow if you don't have internal drive, which is why it's always important to use this strategy to keep you moving forward.

Competitive, but on your own terms

There is no need to be competitive with anyone other than yourself. If you start competing against other people, you are allowing your energy to focus on others as opposed to progressing yourself. I am very competitive about winning but winning according to my vision and my values. I set goals and targets every week throughout my entire career as a trainer, and I still do it today. Anyone who is competitive knows what it's like to win – it feels amazing. But it also fills you with confidence. This in turn makes you want more, which challenges you to set higher goals and targets.

I come from a sporting background. I played rugby for twenty years, and I carried my competitive nature into developing my physique and bodybuilding. I notice a big difference in levels of confidence among coaches who have come from a sporting background versus those who haven't. This is why I am so passionate about helping coaches to develop their bodies as they progress through their careers. (You'll learn this in the Physical sections of the book.)

Start being more competitive with yourself; challenge yourself to accomplish things that you think are hard or set goals that are slightly outside your comfort zone. You'll be amazed how this carries over to the development of your business and your life overall.

Confident in your own abilities

Confidence is an area that many fitness professionals struggle with, and it's an area that will stall your progress if you don't address it. When you are confident, you make clearer decisions, you believe in yourself, and you are also a lot happier. Confidence isn't something that we are all born with; it's an area that you need to work at. So, if you're struggling with low self-confidence at the moment, don't give up and think that you'll have it for life. You can develop confidence.

After coaching hundreds of fitness professionals over the years, I am confident in saying that there are three main areas that will make a dramatic impact in your confidence levels. Firstly, I think it's essential to be a part of a community. By this I mean being around people who have similar passions to yours. As I discussed in the previous section, I grew up playing sports and being surrounded by likeminded friends. We all supported each other to improve and to develop our skills. I transferred this level of community into the fitness world when I qualified. I kept going to courses; every two to three months, I would pay to attend a live course, often in another country. I would spend time in the company of people who shared my passion. Today, it's so easy to sit behind a computer screen and learn. This is helping your knowledge, but it's not improving your personal skills, and it's certainly not confirming whether you actually know the things that you're learning.

I will never forget one particular day when I was on a Poliquin Level 2 course in Sweden. Charles Poliquin was a man who rarely gave out praise; it was very much something that you earned. We were training in the Eleiko Training Centre, and I remember working as hard as I could. I'd been in Charles' presence quite a few times already, and you could always feel his energy when he was standing near you. I was squatting and I remember trying to do it as well as I could. I finished my set and racked the bar. Charles put his hand on my shoulder and said, 'Great set.' I will never forget the surge of confidence that it instilled in me. From that day forward, I have appreciated how valuable it is to be at live educational events.

The majority of my learning throughout my career took place at live events, including seminars, practical coaching workshops and internships. I always made sure that I was surrounded by likeminded coaches. We spent a lot of time together, grew together and worked through plenty of challenges together. My network of fitness industry friends grew – and alongside that, so did my confidence.

PIT STOP

As the internet age continues, don't allow yourself to be confined to your laptop for learning. Take a moment now to think of a community that you could be a part of, be it mentorships, masterminds, practical coaching weekends or live seminars.

Credibility is essential if you want to increase your levels of self-confidence. Why should anyone believe you? You say that you are the coach who can help me to get into the best shape of my life – how can I trust that to be true?

As a coach, one of the main reasons you'll doubt yourself is because you don't have any evidence to support the knowledge that you have. You know you can get people in shape and improve their health or fitness, but you can't show it. Your levels of confidence soar when you have a portfolio of results, but even in if you're the early days of your career you just need your first result to feel the initial surge. If you don't have your first set of results yet, double down your efforts to get it.

I speak to so many coaches who don't record any of their results. It doesn't have to be a body transformation or a photo-shoot client; it can simply be a weight-loss before-and-after picture of your client in street clothes, or a written testimonial from a client accompanied by a photo of them in their street clothes standing next to you in the gym. It can be a video testimonial where your client is describing their experience of working with you. In my early days, I had a small booklet with all my weight-loss results because people who wanted to lose weight were my target audience. Many of my results were written testimonials from my clients, each featuring a picture of me with them by the gym sign. It's so important for your confidence to be able to see a portfolio building, whatever the level of results that you're helping your clients to achieve. Every time you engage with someone who could potentially be a client, you need to have the confidence that you can support your claims.

PIT STOP

Do you know enough? This is a subject that I cover in more detail in the Physical sections of Level Up, but it's also important to cover with regards to confidence and credibility. Are you certified or educated in the subjects that you are talking about? If you're not, what areas of education do you need to invest in?

You will always feel unconfident with subjects that you don't fully understand. Commitment to your education not only increases your credibility – as your potential and current customers can see that you're educating yourself – it also increases your confidence.

Clear thinker

If you're a clear thinker, you know what you want and where you're going. You also know what you need to do to get there. This is closely linked to your vision, something that I highlighted earlier, and an area that few people can say that they have fully nailed down.

If I were to ask you about the direction that your life and your business are going in, could you give me a clear answer? Similarly, if I were to ask you about your clients, who you work with and what area you specialise in, could you answer clearly? Do you make decisions easily, or do you bounce between multiple ideas in your head and become overwhelmed?

These are all questions that you should be asking yourself and working hard to find the answers to. Do your own research on successful people; they are always clear, they know exactly what they want, and they know how they're going to get it.

Are you going to have all the answers today? No. But that doesn't mean you can't get started.

Action taker

A powerful vision and clarity lead to goals and tasks. The only way you are going to achieve your vision and make progress in your business and your life is if you take action. Successful people know what they have to do, and they also commit to doing the work.

One of the most effective ways to ensure that you take the necessary steps is to break down each of your tasks into actions. Then, look at the actions for each task and list them in order of priority. Once you have them listed, go through the linking process that I discussed in the 'Internally driven' section. How does each of the tasks link to the highest of your values? Simply linking your tasks will drive your level of inspiration through the roof, and you'll find yourself taking more action than ever before. Taking action is also one of the best ways to boost your self-confidence. Think how you will feel about yourself if you get to the end of each week and you've ticked off every task on your list that supports the growth and development of your business. You may often get to the end of each week and find you've completed the actions, but you haven't got a measure of your progress. Using a list of tasks and ensuring that you take action on each one becomes your measure. Progress is essential if you want to increase your level of self-confidence.

Analytical

You cannot progress in life and professionally if you don't question where you are now. You should regularly ask yourself whether you are doing enough, what you're missing, and what you have to do in order to be more. You have to consistently question your clients, their results and their progress. It's easy to avoid questioning yourself; that way you don't have any more work to do. However, anyone who wants to achieve anything in their life, those who do want to progress to another level, they're always looking for that extra bit more. That can only come if you learn to question yourself more.

Questions always bring answers, answers give you new areas to action, and action leads to results and ultimately more progress.

Growth minded

Someone who has a growth mindset is driven; they are always looking to learn more; they see failure as an opportunity to grow; and they are committed to self-development. To live with a mindset fixated on continuous development does take a lot of work; however, it's essential if you want to live a life that is constantly moving forward. The opposite of a growth mindset is a fixed mindset. People with fixed mindsets aren't very driven, they struggle to believe that with learning they can improve, and they allow themselves to be affected by opinions, situations and any level of negativity around them.

The interesting thing to note here is that we all have a mixture of both. In her book *Mindset*, Carol Dweck explains that we can't be purely growth minded. There will always be times when we will be challenged by our thoughts, by situations or by other people, and we can end up falling into negativity, self-doubt and limiting belief. These are often the times when we notice slower growth in our lives, both personally and professionally. Growth-minded people, however, can often see this level of doubt coming and are able to switch their level of thinking around.

Growth-minded people often do all they can to protect themselves from environments or situations that challenge their growth mindsets. One of the best ways to do this is to keep company with other growth-minded people.

Optimistic

Building your fitness business takes time – I'm not going to lie and tell you otherwise. There are going to be many challenges along the way, so it's important that you develop an inner confidence. You have to believe that your vision will become a reality. There have been many times when I've not known what to do, or when I've acknowledged that there are some tough times ahead, but I've always remained optimistic. I would always say to myself that as long as I kept ticking off my task-list items and accomplishing my goals, I would always be taking one step closer to my vision. My great friend and International Federation of Bodybuilding and Fitness (IFBB) pro Ben Pakulski gave me a copy of the book *How Champions Think* by Dr Bob Rotella. I will never forget the chapter in it where Dr Rotella discusses the optimism that athletes possess.[5] Large sporting events are often months – in some cases, years – away, but athletes acknowledge that their success will only become a reality if they remain optimistic and positive. Regardless of the challenges that they may face along the way, they believe that all their efforts will pay off come match day.

Passionate

At the time of writing this book, I am nineteen years into my career. I can honestly tell you that I am more passionate about the fitness industry than I was when I started. My passion has grown every single year. One thing that people have always said to me is that my passion shines through when I speak about what I do.

PIT STOP

Think about the last person that you came into contact with who was deeply passionate about what they did. How did they make you feel when you were with them? Passion is infectious – people feel it, and they also can't help but tell other people about it. I explain to people that passion is like fuel to a fire.

I can tell you from experience that the fitness professionals who deliver their craft with deep passion always excel. They have full diaries; they have waiting

---

5   B Rotella, *How Champions Think: In sports and in life* (Simon & Schuster, 2015)

lists and they see the most growth to their businesses over time.

It is, however, easy to lose your passion. I've had a lot of fitness professionals reach out to me over the years and say that they just don't feel the same as when they first started. I always explain the same thing every time: you have to keep your passion alive. You have to learn, and you have to have an internal desire for constant improvement. If you're standing still or going backwards, it's inevitable that you'll feel unfulfilled and begin to question your passion.

It's for this reason that I always suggest committing to some level of education every three months. I also suggest that you attend at least one form of practical education every six months. My whole career has been about growth and education, and it's no surprise that my passion for the fitness industry is as strong as it has ever been.

As you will have realised by now, there is a lot of structure to personal growth. It's all about following habits that are aligned with where you want to go in life and what you want to achieve. Remember that habits, if practised consistently, become a part of you and you end up doing them automatically.

You can't Level Up if you stay the same, which is why I am sharing so many of these strategies and habits with you. Your goal now should be to apply them one by one so that they become a part of you and help you shape your life and business.

You've identified a new and powerful vision, and you should also be well on your way to creating an inspiring set of values for yourself. You should be starting to think about the attributes that you are going to adapt in line with the progress that you want to make. However, there is one further area that I see as the icing on the cake.

What is going to make your vision and values stick? What is going to make you commit to your excellence attributes every single day? You have to change your personal standards. You have to adjust the level of respect that you have for yourself, and you must begin to expect more of yourself.

Creating your personal standards

When someone has written out their vision and set goals to reach, I will always ask them, 'What is going to ensure they get accomplished? What is going to turn your list of tasks into absolute non-negotiables that, no matter what stands in your way, always get done?'

You might have read through some of the excellence attributes and said to yourself, 'I'm not like that. I don't think that's me.' That's because the old version of you is reading them. The version of you who still has lower standards is the version of you who has managed to get to this point in your life. But, as I said in the '10 lessons for fitness professionals' section, this isn't going to be the person who takes you to the next level. It's time to start thinking of yourself as version 2.0.

This is why I want you to identify the standards that you currently hold for yourself, and I want you to set higher standards: the standards that are going to help you to Level Up. To help you to do that, I want to share the impact that personal standards has had on me throughout my career.

Back in my early days, I knew that *the current version of me wasn't going to be the version that was going to take me forward*. On Jane's advice, I attended a three-day event called The Landmark Forum in 2004. Jane said it would be an incredible breakthrough experience for me. I was about to go on a journey to discover what was truly possible in life. The next three days were life changing for me. It's like I had received a brand-new set of eyes, and I was now looking at the world in a different way. I came home a completely different person. I had witnessed an environment where some of the attendees were already operating at a whole different level, and many more were in search of how to get there. What they all had in common was that they were in pursuit of bettering themselves.

This event and Charles Poliquin's seminar in Spain reinforced the importance of standards for me. There weren't any limitations; there was only the highest level of personal standards that seemed to be acceptable. When I came away from both experiences, I wrote down how things were going to change for me. Here are some of my resolutions:

- I was going to wake up positive and grateful for every single day.

- I was going to grow my mind and read every single morning. Previously, I would read sporadically.

- I was going to surround myself with likeminded people. I'd allowed the gym to become the only environment that I spent time in, and I was becoming a reflection of it.

- I was going to travel and learn from the best in the world, no matter how much it cost.

- I was going to take my own body to a level that represented the clients that I wanted to work with. Up to this point, I was training but nowhere near enough to help me see any real change.

- I was going to achieve better results than any coach in my town. Up to this point, I hadn't even set a minimum standard for my results.

This list became my list of non-negotiables. Nothing stood in the way of these being accomplished. The funny thing is that I worked even harder so I could earn the money to travel, and I was getting way better results because I had committed to learning and also travelling. Life was changing at a rapid pace, and it was because I had committed myself 110% to my non-negotiables and they were all aligned with my vision.

Prior to my experiences with Landmark and Charles Poliquin, my actions were completely the opposite. I had allowed myself to start every day with no attempt to control how I was feeling, I surrounded myself with people who didn't share my vision for growth, and I was not training at a high enough level. It was no surprise that I felt so much conflict in my life. I wanted to get somewhere, but my personal standards had to match my vision if I was going to get there.

Over the years, my personal standards continue to move up in line with my values and my vision – my environments, my social circles, and the minimum level of expectations that I have for myself and my life. *For you to grow into the life and business that you want, your personal standards have to change, too.* One of the best ways to achieve this is to go and witness people or businesses who operate with high standards. Spend time in environments where higher standards are on display.

I watched my father as I grew professionally. I became fascinated by the way that he treated people and how he operated his business. I also travelled a lot and spent time being coached by different coaches. I would not only take on board what I was being taught, I took on board their etiquette and their professionalism. I watched the best delivering their crafts, I took what was useful to me, and I discarded what wasn't. I shaped my own personal standards in line with my personality, my values and my vision. I wanted to be known for having high personal standards; I had witnessed how much people stand out when they were operating at a level of excellence.

I used to get the train down to London every few weeks and spend time in hotel bars and coffee shops. I used to watch the delivery and service processes, just soaking up environments where higher standards were on display. Again, I would absorb what aligned well with my vision and discard what didn't. All the while I was developing myself, building layers onto the person and professional that I wanted to be regarded as.

PIT STOP

Are the standards that you currently hold for yourself aligned with the values and vision that you have set? Do you need to spend more time in environments where high personal standards are on display, so that your own can be challenged?

One of the things that I am most proud about in my career to date is the level of personal training that we deliver at M10. Every time a coach comes away from an educational weekend with us or a coaching session at the gym with one of the team, they always refer to the standards that are on display. These are the standards that we work hard to maintain, and we constantly review them.

When you set new personal standards for yourself, you are giving yourself a whole new level to work towards. You are accepting that the level that you want to get to will require a lot more from yourself. You are also accepting that you have to let go of how you were operating in the past so that you can create a new standard for the future.

360 degrees of excellence to Be More!

Take time right now to do a 360 degrees of excellence check in. Ask yourself:

1. Am I growing as a person?
2. Am I developing a better reputation?
3. Are my results where I want them to be?
4. Is my business growing?

I want you to get used to asking yourself these questions. It's so easy to consume information and push on, without acknowledging whether it's having an impact on where you want to get to. If you answer 'no' to one of the above questions at any point, you know that there are areas that you need to action.

Level Up is about progress and stages; it's not about completion. I don't want you to feel overwhelmed at this stage. What I have provided you with in the Personal part of this book is a road map – one that you can use now and work your way through, and one that you can come back to in months to come and use as a reference.

It has taken me a long time to embed everything that you have read in this part of the book into the way that I operate my life, and it's not going to happen for you overnight. You will dip in and out of inspiration and motivation – you're only human. However, as you develop the skills and habits that you have learned, and they become a part of you, you will find it a lot easier to snap yourself out of the dips.

What is important is that you read through and reflect on where you are right now. There might be certain areas, such as a clear vision, that you have firmly imprinted in your mind, yet you are struggling to know how to stay committed to them. In this case, you will find the 'Living your life according to your values' section vital. You might find yourself in an environment that's impacting your energy and pulling you down. You will find that setting a new level of personal standards for yourself will allow you to

Level Up your environments and the company that you keep.

What I love the most about the whole concept of Level Up is that for every level that you rise, your life and your business will improve alongside it. This is your time to grow; you are in control of the chapters that you are writing for your life. Look deep into your vision, write down your values, commit to the excellence attributes, create your list of non-negotiables, and I promise that you'll enjoy progress.

PART TWO
Physical – Learn More!

To help your clients get the best out of themselves, you have to be committed to getting the best out of yourself.

In the Personal sections of *Level Up*, I shared personal experiences to suggest a road map to develop your mind, as well as the habits that will be congruent with your desire to see consistent progress with your life and your business. In this part of the book, I am going to look at the second key area that will support your journey through the fitness industry: your body, your physical development as a fitness professional and the application of your knowledge.

Over the years, I have read and listened to a lot of experienced fitness professionals who have said that how you look is not directly correlated to your coaching ability or level of success. They were saying that the fact that a coach looks good, or is super strong or super fit, doesn't automatically make them a great coach in a specific field.

Those are statements I completely agree with. I have come across a lot of coaches who have had six-packs and phenomenal physiques. They have been able to get themselves in shape, but this has not extended to their coaching ability, their ability to explain their knowledge and their ability to get their clients in shape. I have come across a lot of super-strong strength coaches who train very hard and have dedicated themselves to their sport, but they have limited coaching ability, which is reflected in their lack of coaching accomplishments. Similarly, I have come across coaches who haven't been in shape, yet they possess a lot of knowledge. They have been able to blow my mind with what they know, yet this has not been carried over into the results that they have been able to produce with their clients or even their practical coaching skills.

Having mentored hundreds of coaches personally over the years and educated thousands more with our seminars and practical coaching events, I have witnessed the winning combination many times. I have been fascinated to watch the attributes that successful coaches possess.

What is it that makes them stand out from other coaches?

They have been through the coaching process multiple times; they know what it feels like and they are dedicated to their own physical development. They know what it's like to be coached, and they fully commit to developing a coaching eye. They're invested in not only developing themselves but also in learning how to convey their knowledge to their clients. The best coaches never expect their clients to do something that they haven't done themselves. The best coaches lead from the front and inspire their clients.

So, although someone being in shape isn't a reflection of their coaching ability, *if you combine being in top shape, knowing what it takes to get there, and knowing how to get that across to your clients, that's the winning formula.*

This formula isn't limited to muscle building, weight loss or fat loss. I apply it to coaching endurance sports, strength sports, general fitness, and so on. If you have put yourself where your clients want to get to and even higher, your ability to help someone achieve results is far superior than that of someone who hasn't reached that goal yet.

My belief is clear, and I explain it to coaches like this: Your body is a gift; it is a free canvas to work from. To master your craft, you must not limit your growth to your mind and your knowledge – you must become a true master of your body as well.

PIT STOP

Have you ever been in peak physical shape? Do you know what it's like to excel yourself, to achieve something that you didn't think was ever possible?

We have so many coaches in the fitness industry who struggle with low self-confidence, who struggle to achieve results with their clients, who struggle to talk confidently about their knowledge and who struggle to stand out. I take one look at their own training and the commitment they are making to their physical development, and it's evident that it isn't a high priority.

PIT STOP

Are you in the fitness industry to blend in, or do you want to make a name for yourself? Anyone who wants to make a name for themselves must commit to becoming a master of all areas of their craft.

In this part of the book, I'll be offering you tips to help you Level Up physically. If you follow them, you're not only going to grow in confidence; you will achieve much better results with all of your clients, you will increase your credibility, you will build your reputation a lot quicker and you will grow your business. If you're not in shape right now, or you haven't been in your best shape yet, now is the time for you to take your physical fitness to the next level – not only to look good, but also for what it will teach you and how it will carry over to your coaching.

Commit to the journey

Have you ever been fully disciplined with your diet and training? Do you know what it's like to follow a plan for a period of time and not slip off track? To be tempted to go out partying or miss a training session but choose to resist the temptation and commit to the task at hand?

Every day as a coach you are asking your clients to stick to their plan, focus and commit to their goals. Of course, not all of them do, but do you really know what they're experiencing? Are you able to relate to their struggles if you've never been through them yourself?

When my weight-loss clients would tell me how hard it was to not drink at social events, I would tell them the tricks that I used to make it look like I had an alcoholic drink when I didn't. I never restricted my social life when I was losing weight, and I knew how important it was for them, too, so I was able to relate to every situation and provide them with tools to keep them on track.

When guys who are trying to add muscle tell me that they're struggling to get their meals in, and they complain that it's too many calories, I know exactly what that feels like. I know what it's like to be sat in front of a meal and to be so full I felt like I was bursting, but I knew I had to just get the food in. I had seen my weight fall as a result of not eating enough, so I could relate to my clients when they were struggling, too.

When clients used to tell me that they had no energy deep into a diet and that it was getting too much for them, I knew exactly what they were going through. For a lot of coaches, this is the time when you feel sorry for your clients and allow them to ease off. That's because you haven't been where they are, so you don't expect any more of them. Because I'd been there many times, I knew that they needed to suck it up and push that extra bit harder. I didn't let them give in; I'd expected more of myself and so I expected it from them, too. As a coach, it's important that your instructions come from an authentic place, not a place that you're trying to imagine.

You might be reading this and saying to yourself, 'How does this carry over to your weight-loss clients? You haven't been heavily overweight, Mark, so how do you know how it feels for someone in that position?'

From my perspective, discipline is discipline; it doesn't matter if you have 36lbs to lose or 10lbs to lose. Yes, there will be different psychological factors that you might have in front of you, but for many years I used my own discipline and journey to relate to many of my weight-loss clients. I've been well over 20% body fat at one point in my life and regained control of my body. I've also added 40kg to my physique by being disciplined and relentlessly committed.

My clients would regularly reference the discipline that I showed in my bodybuilding and my commitment to develop my physique, and they would always tell me that it was inspiring to them. I would explain to them why I had discipline. I had identified that my goal was important to me, just like I explained in the linking exercise in the 'Living your life according to your values' section. It was my job to help my clients link the importance of their goal to the discipline that they needed to be able to reach it. I was able to use my journey to relate to them.

You are your clients' leader. When you lead your clients from the front, they will follow; when you show discipline, your clients will always be inspired by your actions. What do your clients think when they know that you don't really train, when they know that you don't follow a diet or have any goals? Do you think that creates any challenge for them? Of course it does. As a coach, I believe that to teach discipline you must show that you have it, too.

Think about your portfolio and reputation. Are you going to be known as someone who achieves results if none of your clients are displaying any level of discipline? The more discipline I displayed throughout my career, the more it impacted my reputation and what people would say about me. People would arrive at a consultation knowing about me; they would know that I expected a lot of myself and of my clients, and they knew that discipline would play a big part in the programme that they were about to start.

You have the opportunity to instil behaviours and beliefs in your clients with your own actions. This is why it's so important that you commit to your own journey and experience everything that you expect of your clients.

Hire a coach

Have you ever been coached? To be a true master of your craft, you must experience high-level coaching. How can you Level Up if you have no level to aspire to? In my early days as a coach, I genuinely thought that I was developing at a fast pace – I thought my coaching standard was way higher than it actually was.

For the majority of coaches reading this book, you'll be the best coach at your facility, so naturally you're going to think you're more skilled than everyone else. It's likely that the rest of the coaches are asking you for advice all the time. This isn't going to help you to

Level Up. You need to allow yourself to be a small fish in a big pond.

Would it surprise you to learn that nearly 90% of the coaches that have passed through our practical coaching courses hadn't received any form of professional coaching until they attended our event? When asked to take someone through an exercise in front of the rest of the group the majority of coaches would panic, simply because they'd never been challenged before. Every coach who receives coaching for the first time will always tell me that it's been a complete game changer for them. They say it's like they've been given a new set of eyes.

My first experience of high-level coaching was at my Level 1 Poliquin certification. The attention to detail while we were training was beyond anything I'd ever seen before. I knew I hadn't been coaching like that. I read over the programmes that we had been given and they were so different to what I'd been writing.

As soon as I got back to my gym, my coaching changed. I became more attentive with my clients, and I was more detailed with my programming. Because we'd been pushed hard through our workouts at the certification, I started to expect more from my clients, as well.

The same thing happened when I came back from my Level 2 certification. I'd got myself into a slightly comfortable situation at my gym, and I really noticed it when we were taken through our certification training sessions. Yet again, I acknowledged that I could pay a lot more attention to my clients, and I knew my programmes could be better and that I could push myself harder in the gym.

This is why I am so keen to recommend practical coaching workshops or hiring your own coach. Your practical coaching and your own training will not be impacted if you only try to educate and evaluate yourself online. After two practical courses, it was clear to me that I could take my own training to another level if I hired my own coach to be accountable to. I worked with Luke Leaman for a period of time and then went on to hire IFBB Pro John Meadows.

While I worked with both coaches, I pushed myself harder than I ever had before because I had a level of accountability. My diet was written for me, and my programmes were delivered in three-month blocks. My strength went through the roof as a result of following their programmes, and I added more muscle than ever before; but, above everything, my confidence shot up.

I was learning about programming and how the coaches were adjusting my diet as we went along. They were assessing my physique and giving me regular feedback, which helped me to understand more about what they were looking for when they saw my pictures.

Every time I questioned whether we could make any more progress, they provided me with the next step that took me even further forward. This always gave me another level of self-belief, but it also carried over to the clients that I was coaching. My clients were seeing my progress visibly, but I also found it valuable to explain what I was doing with my training. Whenever they would feel like complaining, they would always know how hard I was working.

Alongside the online coaching that I was receiving, I attended more and more practical coaching courses all around the world. Each time there were different coaches, and I got to experience different styles of coaching. They would always pick up on specific areas to help me with my eye for detail, my effort, my understanding of exercises or even correcting some of my techniques. I would watch each coach and make notes on the delivery of their sessions. Were they hands on with their clients? When were they pushing for a little bit more effort, and when had they decided that a set was over?

I can't stress enough how important it is to watch other coaches and to *receive* 121 coaching. You will be blind to so much that goes on during a coaching session or throughout a coaching process if you haven't had it pointed out to you.

For example, when observing coaches, I always say to the coaches, 'Please tell me when you see an issue that someone else is having, as I want to be able to see it, too.' They tell me when they see the back rounding during a squat, or the chest not being recruited effectively during a dumbbell press. They explain what they see on each person, why it was happening and how to correct it. They show me when someone wasn't working hard enough and explain how to get more from the exercise being performed.

I will never forget spending over a month in Tampa, training alongside my friend Ben Pakulski as he prepared for the Arnold Classic bodybuilding show in 2015. I learned so much from watching him train – his attention to detail, his work ethic, and the invaluable tips that he shared about my own training and how to improve my coaching.

The best thing about hiring a coach or receiving coaching is that the coach has been where you are right now. They've put in thousands of coaching hours. They know more than you because they've either studied more, they've applied themselves more or they've been in the industry a lot longer. They can see everything that you can't, and they can help you fast track your career by pointing out what you'd otherwise have to work out for yourself.

I had various different coaches throughout my career. Each one had a different coaching style; some would support me more in terms of emails on a week-to-week basis, and some would let me get on and ask me to get in touch when I needed them. Some would expect me to travel to them in order to learn how to train more efficiently. I flew overseas on multiple occasions when I was being coached by IFBB Pro Milos Sarcev. I would also travel to different parts of the country to train with my great friend Jordan Peters when he was coaching me.

Some of my coaches would send detailed programmes; some would send them in a short email. I evaluated the coaching style of every coach that I worked with, the parts that I liked and parts that I didn't think aligned with me. Every coach that I've ever worked with had an impact on how I coach people today.

As you'll learn in the Professional sections, your coaching style and level of support will be reflective of your brand standards, the customer experience that you want to create and your brand values. Watching other coaches work allows you to review your own standards and helps you to shape the coaching business and reputation that you want moving forward. *You can't improve as a coach and as a professional if the only person you're measuring yourself against is you.*

Throughout the first ten years of my career, the majority of my income went back into attending practical coaching courses, hiring coaches to work with me and mentoring. I was never worried about my level of investment because every time I reached out to someone, either my confidence shot up, my results improved, my income increased, or my reputation grew.

Level Up is about taking steps towards excellence. It's about the progress that you make, and hiring a coach is one of the best ways to take your coaching to the next level.

Develop a coaching eye

When I observe any coach at work, I look for one specific thing: the coaching eye. Do you have the ability to watch your clients as they perform exercises and see what's going on? There are coaches who simply help their clients to have a workout and that's all they focus on, and then there are coaches who are constantly looking for ways to help their clients improve throughout each coaching session.

Throughout a training session, a coach who has a keen coaching eye is looking at multiple things at once. They're not just looking at how hard their client is training; they're looking at the exercise itself, if it's being performed correctly, how and if it can be progressed, and the areas where they can add more value during rest times in between exercises. A coach with a keen coaching eye is someone who has progression, results and professional delivery firmly on their mind at all times.

A coach who isn't constantly looking out for change is a coach who isn't interested in progress. I always want to know why something is the case, and when I don't know why I go in search of the answer. Every single time I've received an answer to a why, my clients have progressed, my results have improved and so has my business.

There are five foundational pillars that I am always looking for when I'm coaching someone: posture, stability, execution, strength and effort. These will give you a road map as you develop your coaching eye.

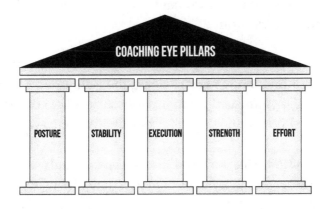

Posture: At the start of your personal training career, you will have learned about *posture*. However, I see coaches allowing their clients to perform exercises with terrible posture (rounded shoulders and over-arching the lumbar spine, for example). If you see poor posture, you need to correct it.

Stability: Are your clients strong enough to be performing unstable exercises? Do they have enough *stability*? At the start of my career, I would ask my clients to perform exercises such as lunges and I would always be confused if they couldn't do them. The desire to always ask why led me to stability. They simply weren't stable enough to do them yet. The muscles surrounding the hip were so weak, every time they performed the exercise they would struggle to return back to the starting position. (I'm sure you've seen this yourself many times.) Again, the keen coaching eye told me that something wasn't right, so I regressed my clients to exercises that they could perform safely and progress from.

When your client always looks like they're in control of their body, they're doing the right exercise for them. If your client is falling over or unable to control themselves or the load, it's not right for them (yet).

Execution: This is a word that has been popularised in the fitness industry in recent years. It relates to how an exercise is performed, if the correct muscles are being used throughout, and if there is the correct amount of tension placed upon the muscle(s) throughout each exercise. There is a lot more to exercise than what is printed on the tutorial cards stuck to the sides of machines; yet, that's where a lot of coaches seem to take their execution knowledge from.

I'm sure you will have looked at your clients performing certain exercises and thought they didn't look right, but you've just pushed on regardless. A coach who has a keen coaching eye and an understanding of exercise execution will constantly be watching each exercise as it's performed. They'll know what the exercise should look like when it's executed correctly, which muscle(s) should be performing the exercise, and where tension is placed upon the muscle(s), and they'll be thinking of ways to help their clients to progress when they reach the end of each set.

Your clients will often tell you when they can and can't feel a muscle working. In fact, I'm sure you can say the same for your own training. This isn't your cue to push on; this is where you should be digging into your execution tool kit to provide a solution. Each exercise has a number of teaching cues, which are a set of instructions that will help your clients to learn each movement. They also help your clients maintain maximal tension within the working muscle(s) throughout each set.

Exercise execution is extremely valuable when it comes to the progression of exercises. The goal of introducing any exercise is to get your client to perform it perfectly before you progress. In doing so, your client will be using the correct muscles, they will be in full control of the exercise and they will be ready to progress through each stage of their training journey.

If you've never been coached by an expert in exercise execution, you'll struggle to get the most out of your clients, and you certainly won't know what you should be looking out for. I believe that everyone has progress in them – it's our jobs as coaches to show them what's truly possible.

Strength: When it comes to the next pillar, *strength*, I see way too many coaches failing to progress their clients. Strength is essential for weight/fat loss, physique development and sports performance, and it's also crucial for day-to-day performance, health and longevity. Until you start to focus on strength as a measure of progress, you'll never appreciate how much your clients value it as a motivational measure.

To use strength as a variable and to support your clients' levels of progress, you can look for an increase in load used on a particular exercise over time or an increase in the number of reps performed with a specific load, or you could look to vary the rep ranges that you use across a workout or through specific stages of the coaching process.

All of your clients have the ability to improve their strength. A coach who has a keen coaching eye will be using strength as a measure for progression. It might not be at every session, but it will always play a part in the coaching thought process.

Effort: The final pillar. Just like strength, your clients have all got more effort to give. However, in a lot of cases they have no idea what level of effort is required to achieve the results they've said that they want. So, throughout the coaching process you have to *show* effort in order to get the maximum effort out of your clients.

Remember: the coaching process is a two-way street. You can't just expect your client to be the only one who is putting effort in. You might be having a busy day, your client might be the last session of the day or you might have things going on outside of the gym, but for the duration of the coaching session you have to give your client everything that you've got.

Don't confuse effort with smashing your clients into the ground; that's not professional coaching. When I say 'effort', what I mean is getting a little bit more out of your clients every time they train with you – watching to see if there is an extra rep at the end of a set, or if your client is trying to rest longer than necessary. You might think these things aren't important, but you only achieve results because of increased effort which is repeated over time. If your clients are training with the same level of effort three months into their programme, you will have missed out on a great deal of progress that they could have made.

The person you are today isn't the same person who is going to achieve the end result. Your habits have to change, your mindset has to change and the level of effort that you put into your training has to change.

As a coach, it is your responsibility to drive the effort and intensity as your client progresses along their journey. A coach who has a keen coaching eye has a global overview of what their client is doing throughout a coaching session. As well as being personable and continuing to develop the client-and-coach relationship (your client's training session doesn't need to be boring), you always need to have your eye on posture, stability, execution, strength and effort.

The education journey

After reading the 'Developing a coaching eye' section, you might be questioning whether you have one and (hopefully) wondering how you can develop one. Some of the pillars might have resonated with you, and others may be new areas that you know you need to work on. Maybe you already know about all of the pillars, but you're just not utilising and applying what you know.

As this book is all about levelling up, I want to provide you with all the necessary tools so that you can progress across all areas. This will only happen if you learn to question yourself constantly. However, you have little to question if you don't know what you're looking for. Many of you will work on your own, and if you work within a team you might not discuss your education and professional development on a regular basis with your co-workers.

In this section, I'm going to share a list of the subjects that I believe every coach needs to know more about. Do you have to be an expert in all of them? No, not at all, but you need to understand them if you want to help your clients make progress. You also need to know about them if you want to develop your reputation, achieve better results and progress your career.

Continually developing your education throughout your career gives you a new way of looking at each of your clients. I remember studying with the Institute of Functional Medicine (IFM) in Florida in 2011, and right at the start the lecturer said that we would have a new set of eyes by the end of the three days. This resonated with me because I knew there was so much more that I could be doing to help my clients – I just couldn't see what. When I came back and started asking my clients more questions, I was able to understand so much more than before.

It's important to note that a great fitness professional will always refer out when faced with something that is out of their scope of practice. The team at M10 and I have a large range of specialists that we refer out to. Not only is this expected – because you are not qualified to heal or diagnose anything for your clients – but working alongside other professionals is also highly respected by your clients. You will learn a great deal when you work with other professionals, and you will also get the opportunity to see how they operate their businesses. I encourage every coach that I work with to build relationships with a private doctor (ideally functional medicine trained), osteopath, physiotherapist and chiropractor.

In fact, when I worked in a health club and moved into my first personal training studio, one of my greatest referral relationships was with a local physiotherapist. I was having treatment every two weeks as a maintenance protocol alongside my training, and through each session we would regularly talk about my coaching and subjects relating to the body. As my physiotherapist started to learn more about my work, I could tell that she was beginning to trust me. It started with one referral and then progressed over the course of four to five years. When you work with another professional, it's not just a case of what you'll learn; it's also a case of what you'll earn and how it will support the development of your business.

As you go through the subjects in this section, I want you to think about your clients and ask yourself how an increase in knowledge of each particular field could help your clients progress. You have a portfolio of clients, and there is always something that you can be researching or working on that will help them in their journey.

Anatomy and physiology

One of the first questions that I will ask a coach is whether they know their anatomy and physiology

(A&P). Do you understand what it is that you work on every single day? It's not uncommon for coaches to say that the last time they looked into A&P was when they sat their personal training qualifications or university degree. So, when faced with a question as simple as, 'Show me where the pec major originates and inserts', they look completely baffled.

Here's something that is vital for you to understand: You are being hired to help someone to improve their body shape, strength, fitness and health. To do that, your clients have to perform exercises, which requires the use of muscles, bones, joints, ligaments and tendons. This might sound like I'm being patronising – I assure you that I'm not; this knowledge is sadly overlooked by a large percentage of coaches.

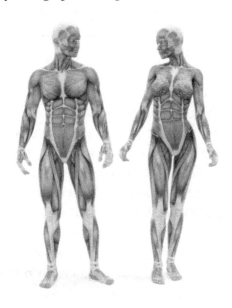

The beginning of the coaching process should involve an assessment. This will include a visual assessment of your client's posture, some form of flexibility assessment and a movement-based assessment. When you look at your clients, do you honestly know what you're looking at? When you see internally rotated shoulders or an excessive anterior tilted pelvis, do you know which muscles could be tight, strong or weak? If you do, do you know where they originate and insert? Understanding the origin and insertion of muscles allows you to understand which direction muscles and their associated fibres run in (more of this in the 'Biomechanics' section). This, in turn, allows you to understand which direction certain muscles could be pulling the associated joints in. Knowing this information will provide you with a certain pool of exercises to begin using with your clients, and also a pool of exercises that you would avoid until later into your client's journey.

When you are speaking to your clients about their assessments, a solid understanding of A&P will allow you to clearly explain what you have seen, which educates them and fills them with confidence in themselves. This is why displaying high levels of confidence in your own knowledge and coaching ability is a powerful professional attribute.

As a coach, you will place your hands on your clients with the intention of guiding them to perform each exercise in the correct fashion, and also to ensure that they are using the right muscles. It's clear to see in many cases that coaches don't know which muscles are being used, as their hands are often in the wrong places.

As I explained in the 'Hire a coach' section, this is where practical experience of working with a skilled coach or attending practical courses is crucial. It's one thing seeing A&P in books, but it's completely different when someone shows it to you in a practical situation.

If you're training someone who is looking to develop their physique, it is essential for you to know your A&P as your primary goal is muscular development. When looking at a physique, you will see a variance in muscle belly insertion points – some will attach very low and some will attach very high onto the tendon. When you are able to look at muscle belly insertion points, you will have a clearer understanding of someone's genetic ability to develop muscle tissue in that area. The difference between having short and long insertion points mostly impacts the presentation of the muscle when developed. Your clients will often be inspired by their favourite physique athletes; however, it's important to make them aware that everyone is different. It's likely that they will have a very different structure to those of their idols (which includes muscle belly insertions), and as such their ability to develop their physique and how it will be presented will be different. You will only know this and be able to explain it to your clients if you know your A&P.

When you are helping someone to develop their physique, it is also important for you to be able to see which muscles are underdeveloped. When you know your A&P, you will be able to break down which of the quad muscles are smaller or larger in comparison; and you'll see if the lower lats are less developed than the upper, if the short head of the biceps is less developed than the long, and if the upper pecs are less developed than the lower. These are just a few examples, but the point is that being able to identify where someone's physique is weaker will carry over to how you design their programme and what you will see when they perform exercises on the gym floor. I will often look over programmes that have been written for physique development, and they do not correlate with the physical structure of the client that they have been created for.

Again, all of this might seem simple, but even the most 'advanced' or 'experienced' coaches struggle to explain what they are looking at. A lot of coaches become lazy as they progress through their careers; this is often due to working alone. If you have been working on your own for a long time, and you haven't had anyone looking over your shoulder, take a moment to reflect on whether you have been keeping up with your A&P.

I have a few recommendations to take your A&P up a level. The first thing I would do is purchase an A&P textbook or – even easier – go and find the one that you used when you studied for your qualifications. For a month, commit to going over each region of the body and testing yourself every day. Don't study anything else during this month. I would suggest you sit down with the textbook open and look through a selection of your client's assessment photos. Look at what you see in the pictures and then look at what the book is showing you. I don't know of a coach who has been through this process and hasn't had their passion for the human body and for their clients reignited. We are privileged to be able to work on such magnificent structures and to help people to improve the quality of their lives.

PIT STOP

I often speak to coaches who say that they have got a bit stale and have started to find coaching boring. I ask them, 'What are you studying at the moment, and what have you studied in the last six months?' If you're not learning, you'll be stagnating.

Every client provides an opportunity for you to learn because everyone is different. It's no wonder you have become stale if you're not committing to learning as you coach. This is even more reason to get your head back into the books.

The second thing you can do is put an anatomy chart up in your assessment room at the gym where you work, or on the wall at home. Whenever you conduct an in person or online assessment, use your anatomy chart as a reference. Look at what you are seeing on your client, and then look in detail at the chart. When you are working with a client in person, they always find it interesting when you point out what you see on them – especially when they might have an injury or aches and you are able to point out which muscle(s) are being affected. It's true in our field that if you don't use it you will lose it, and this definitely applies to anatomy. Having a chart in your eyesight all the time helps you to keep on top of your A&P.

Finally, one of the most valuable experiences of my career was booking myself onto a cadaver day (in fact, I have done it twice). This was an incredible opportunity to study anatomy on a dead body. Over two days, alongside other professionals, we dissected a human body and researched everything from skin to fascia, bones and each individual muscle. Working on a human body truly takes studying A&P to a whole new level as you see things that a textbook will never be able to replicate. You respect the depth that muscle sits within the body and the complexity of all the muscles that originate and insert around complex joints such as the hips and shoulders.

You might be thinking that this is taking research a little too far, and I've had a good number of coaches ask me over the years why I went to these lengths to learn. As a coach, and someone who works with the human body every single day, I wanted to know my craft inside out. We are trusted by our clients every day to help them to improve in all areas – physical development being one of the main ones. I'm sure you'll agree that there are many things that you see every day that baffle you. I didn't want to feel baffled when I was coaching my clients; I wanted to be able to clearly and concisely explain what I could see and provide them with a programme that helped them to progress. If I don't provide you with levels that you can progress to as a coach, you have no marker to work from. Over the years, it's quite likely that your coaching has dropped down a few levels, and it's even more likely that you won't have noticed, so having a few gentle reminders of areas that you've been overlooking will always give your coaching and business a boost.

Biomechanics

Biomechanics follows on perfectly from A&P as it refers to the science of human movement. I've explained the importance of knowing what you're looking at when you are assessing your clients; the next level is understanding and appreciating how muscles, bones, ligaments and tendons all come together to create movement. You often see one thing when you look at your client statically (in the assessment room), and then it all changes when they start to move – when force (load) is applied to the body, as in when exercises are performed, or when your body comes into contact with the ground, such as when running.

In the 'Developing a coaching eye' section, I said that skilled coaches have a passion for knowing why certain things happen. When you're coaching your clients, do you often see things and think that they just don't look right? Have you ever given a client an exercise and they can't do it (or feel the correct muscles), no matter what you do or say? Now, do you think you'd be able to help them to improve if you knew what was supposed to be happening?

Instead of looking for the why, a lot of coaches keep trying to do the same exercises over and over in the hope that repetition will solve the issue. This is one of the main reasons why your clients stagnate, which also leads to a lot of frustration (for you and for them). If your clients don't feel like they're making progress, they'll often start to ask other people for their opinions or advice. The more conflicted they become, the more likely it is that they'll end the coaching relationship with you (sometimes with an excuse, like that they can't afford it). I'm sure you've experienced this.

One of the main reasons I started to question my coaching in the early days is because I could tell how frustrated my clients were getting when they weren't progressing. I was asking them to do exercises that they weren't ready for, and I didn't realise it; I just hoped that they would improve as we went through the coaching process. I want to remind you at this point that wherever you are in your career right now, I've been there too. I didn't just skip the coaching mistakes that everyone makes; I had to learn just like you.

As a coach, my goal is to see my clients continually moving forward. As my career progressed, I'd regularly end up with a client for over three years and they'd be making some level of progress at every session. If you're reading this and thinking, 'How is that possible?' know that it came down to how well I knew my client's body, how interested I was in my clients, how I had programmed my client's exercises and the education that I was providing for them along the way. So, if you're struggling with your clients right now, don't give up – there's another level that you can go to. You just need to start asking more questions and then commit to finding the answers.

A coach who is skilled and understands biomechanics will have a clear understanding of exercise execution (the way we perform an exercise), how muscles are supposed to be recruited when performing an exercise/movement (movement execution), and stabilisation (how to maintain control of the body, both statically and dynamically). They will also be able to appreciate and understand forces and loading that occur (to joints and muscles) through movement and exercise, such as when the heel strikes the ground when running or when a machine chest press is performed.

As I mentioned in the 'Developing a coaching eye' section, in recent years the term 'exercise execution' has become popular in the physique development world, with many people assuming that biomechanics simply refers to how exercises are performed on machines or when dumbbells/barbells are used. But it's important to remember that biomechanics is the analysis of human movement. If your clients are recreational runners, play a sport, or want to lose weight or develop their physiques, understanding biomechanics will help them to minimise injury risk and enable them to perform at their best, whatever their goal.

I was first introduced to biomechanics back in 2008 when I studied the work of Gary Gray (a respected physical therapist from the US). I studied a system that he created which looked at the body as a 'chain reaction' (the idea that the body works as one complete unit).[6] We were taught to understand what was happening to every joint and muscle as the body moved through gait (walking), and then throughout exercise. To this day, it is one of the most complicated courses that I have ever taken (six months of work just to learn the content), but it gave me a brand-new set of eyes. I was able to appreciate how muscles create force and movement, how the body creates stability around joints, how and why muscular imbalances occur, and how to create optimal muscle recruitment through movement and exercise. This allowed me to

---

6   Gary Gray, Functional Video Digest Series, www.grayinstitute.com/
     store/category/10/dvds-functional-video-digest-series

see what was going wrong when I looked at exercise/ movement being performed. It also gave me a road map to create effective programming, which also helped my clients to make a great deal of progress.

For hours, those of us on the course would sit and watch our case studies walk up and down a room, highlighting to our assessor what we were able to see. For example, when the left heel hit the ground in gait, we had to know what the muscles were doing at the same time around the opposite scapula. When our case studies were performing an exercise such as the barbell bench press, we had to explain what was happening to the muscles and joints around the chest. After all, the body works as a complete unit; muscles don't work in isolation. Why am I telling you this? Because the reason why you're not progressing at the rate that you'd like to is perhaps because you're not investing enough time into your education. You can't see what other skilled and experienced coaches can see.

Later into my career, I was introduced to Resistance Training Specialist (RTS – founded by Tom Purvis) by my friend Ben Pakulski. The certification largely focuses on exercise mechanics, which, to quote from the RTS website is, 'an application of engineering and physics to the understanding, implementation, and delivery of exercise'.[7] While Gary Gray's course

7   Resistance Training Specialist (RTS) www. resistancetrainingspecialist.com, accessed February 2020

helped me to understand biomechanics and human movement, I was at a stage in my career where I was looking to learn more about exercise execution. There were many times when, despite my knowledge of biomechanics and movement, I couldn't get my clients (or myself, for that matter) to feel certain muscles. I couldn't understand why certain exercises would feel good and why there were others that I just couldn't connect with (I'm sure you can relate to this). I didn't want to accept this; I wanted to know why. Because the RTS certification looks at the role that physics and mechanics play in how we perform exercises (especially gym-based ones), it was able to give me the answers. With what I learned, I was able to feel muscles like never before and I had a new set of coaching tools to help my clients make more progress, which transferred into the results that I was able to produce.

Unlike a lot of courses that coaches take today, a large percentage of my education throughout my career has been practical. This meant that I was often sat with someone while I was being taught, and they were looking over my shoulder as I was applying what I was learning. The benefit of this was that I was able to ask for advice relating to the issues that I was facing with my own clients. With learning purely online, you're left to apply what you've learned on your own. How you have interpreted the material will determine how you apply it and whether it has a positive impact on your results and the progression of your coaching business. This is one of the main reasons why a large percentage of the education that my team and I provide through M10 is practical.

Studying biomechanics and exercise mechanics is a complete game changer for any coach, and I'm grateful that I was introduced to it so early in my career. It doesn't matter if you work with athletes, weight-loss clients, physique development or injury prevention – when you understand and can apply biomechanics into your coaching, your results will go to the next level.

Psychology and human behaviour

It's likely that you're unaware how important psychology and human behaviour is to fitness coaching, and, as we discussed with biomechanics, you will find yourself repeating your advice week after week in the hope that the penny will drop for your clients.

PIT STOP

How many more results do you think you'd have with your clients if they were able to stick to their plans? Do you often feel you're banging your head against a brick wall, trying to understand why your clients do some of the things that they do?

It's important to understand that your clients will often say one thing and do another; this is simply down to their lack of awareness and understanding. They have patterns of behaviour and emotions (feelings that influence their behaviour) that have been developed over many years. In order for them to make any level of progress with you, any faulty patterns and behaviours have to be addressed and replaced with new ones that are conducive to the results that they want to achieve. It's vital to understand that your clients are unaware that their daily actions and emotions are often unaligned with what is required for them to make a change.

Every client that you coach is different; this is why some of them will do well from day one with very little direction and others seem to need a lot more from you – and even then, they still seem to struggle. A skilled coach will be able to analyse their clients from the consultation process through to the initial coaching stages. They will be able to create a road map which will be appropriate for where their client is at that moment.

PIT STOP

Are your daily actions always in line with your goals?

I ask the Pit Stop question above because to be able to help your clients with their behaviour and emotions, you need to be in control of your own. I come across so many coaches who struggle with their own diets, lack the ability to stick to their training, and struggle to understand which direction their own lives are going in. Look at the discipline that you put into your education and development, or the detail that you put into each of your clients' case studies – do you lack consistency from time to time?

Behaviour is behaviour, consistency is consistency, and therefore you and your clients will often be struggling with similar things. Understanding this completely changed how I approached coaching my clients, and it changed the level of results that I achieved. Taking control and understanding my clients started with me. This is why I shared so much information about myself in the Personal sections.

Training is no different; the more you appreciate how training feels to your own body, the easier you will find it to teach to your clients. So many coaches study psychology and behaviour and have no appreciation of what change really feels like. The more you use yourself as a canvas to learn on, the better your relationships will be with your clients.

As you read through this section, please take time to reflect on yourself and your day-to-day actions. After all, one of the most powerful ways to get your clients to stick to their plan is by leading by example.

I remember back in 2005, I stood next to my client on the treadmill as she warmed up (yes, I've done it, too). She was telling me how she hadn't managed to stick to the diet that I had written out for her (yet again), and I remember being frustrated. Every week we seemed to have the same conversation and we weren't getting anywhere. Instead of waiting another week to hear the same, I decided to do some more research.

I came across the work of a nutritionist named Jonny Bowden, and he had a DVD programme (I'm showing my age here) called 'The Truth About Weight Loss!'[8] One of the main things I took away from his short course is that diets are often too hard for our clients to follow. Armed with this information, I went back to my client and asked her if she thought that her diet was hard to follow, to which she said 'yes'. I then asked her what she thought she could stick to. We found a happy medium, I provided her with a lot more variety and a little less food, and she suddenly started to follow her diet. As a result, she started to lose weight and she was also enjoying following the plan for the first time. This was when I learned about coach and client communication, but I also learned how individualised I was going to have to make each of my client relationships. Until we start talking to our clients, learning more about them and listening to them, we have no idea what challenges they're facing. In this case, my client was only being resistant because I was providing her with the same nutritional protocol that I gave to all my other clients. In order for her to start making progress, I had to make her plan a lot easier for her to fit into her life, I had to lower

---

8   Jonny Bowden, 'The Truth About Weight Loss!' [DVD]

the quantity of food that I had asked her to have, and she needed a lot more variety. For a long time, simply because I was disciplined with my diet, I expected my clients to be the same. In this case, I had to put myself in my client's shoes and understand where she was currently at on her fat-loss journey.

This is where psychology and human behaviour comes into the equation. You need to know what to listen out for, what questions to ask and what action to take with the information that you receive. Often during general conversation with your clients you'll hear things, but because you're unaware of what to listen for you will miss vital information.

If we use weight-loss clients as an example, there is often an emotional story to weight gain. There might have been a relationship break up at some stage in your client's life, the loss of someone close to them, or even challenging memories from their childhood. These events can cause people to retain their weight no matter what diet you give them, and they'll only be able to progress if the emotional attachment that they're holding onto is addressed. Because no one has been able to connect the dots for them, year after year they've been going back and forth trying every diet under the sun.

A client of mine kept losing weight and then regaining it. No matter what I did and how much I supported her with her diet, the same pattern kept repeating itself.

My client was becoming more frustrated by the day, and it clearly wasn't her fault. She didn't understand the pattern that was being created and was starting to consider alternative options to help her keep the weight off. There was clearly an emotion that my client was experiencing between the stages of losing the weight and regaining it. I asked her if she could tell me about the last time in her life when she lost a considerable amount of weight. Interestingly, the last time she was smaller was at a time in her life when she perceived herself to be very unhappy (she experienced an unhappy relationship). I asked her if she would like to be feeling like that again, and she said, 'No way, I never want to feel like that again.' Now we had a link: she wants to lose the weight, but she doesn't want to be unhappy again. So, every time she starts to do well and lose weight, her subconscious emotions take control and sabotage all of her hard work to prevent her feeling the unhappy emotions again. This is a classic case of emotions being in control – something that she was completely unaware of.

Armed with the coaching techniques that I had learned from Dr Demartini, I asked this client to consider looking back at the time when she perceived herself to be unhappy. Even though she wanted to focus on the downsides of that time in her life, there were also going to be a lot of benefits. When we spoke in depth about that time, she started to tell me how she had moved right after it, and that she started the best job she'd ever had, and how she met new friends.

Within a year, her new friends had introduced her to her now fiancé, which she said wouldn't have happened if she hadn't moved. I sat with her going over this time in her life, and the list of positive benefits that came from that one unhappy moment kept growing. When I asked her if that 'unhappy' time in her life was actually all that bad, she said, 'No, completely not.' She actually said that it was a great time in her life, and that she had never thought of it as such. You see, often we perceive something to be one way until we choose (or we are shown how) to look at it in another way. The majority of us are carrying around so much tangled-up emotion, it's preventing us from living a truly fulfilling life and being able to take action on our goals. This is one example of how managing emotions helped my client to break out of the weight-loss cycle that she had been in for years.

I am creating each part and section in *Level Up* to give you a new set of eyes – a new way to be able to look at your clients – and also to highlight many key areas of coaching that you might have overlooked. Your job as a coach is to commit to never-ending education, because at the other side of new knowledge is every opportunity to change.

I didn't know what I know now when I started, or even five years into my career. But I always had that question, why, at the forefront of my mind. Your clients aren't stagnating because they're stubborn, or they don't want to listen to you; they simply lack the knowledge, skill and action necessary to achieve their results. *As a coach, you have an incredible gift, the ability to learn, and then, with your knowledge, the ability to impact the lives of thousands throughout your career.*

It's important at this stage to acknowledge that you are not a psychologist, so you are not qualified to diagnose or treat. If you come across a client who informs you that they have a diagnosed psychological disorder, then you must refer out. However, you are able to learn, and that will make you better informed to tailor your coaching to your client's specific behaviours, emotions and actions. When you listen to your clients and ask questions, patterns always emerge. These tangled patterns are often the reason why your clients are struggling to make progress. But remember, if you have similar tangled-up emotions, you'll struggle to see them in others. This is why working on yourself is just as important as learning about your clients' behaviours.

I haven't attempted to talk about psychology or human behaviour in detail because it's such a complex subject, and because I am not a psychologist or a professor of psychology. I have been studying the subject for over fifteen years and I still learn something new every day. In fact, I still have mentors who support me with my own personal development. I simply want to get you started if you haven't looked into this field and give you the opportunity to Level Up in this area, which will have a dramatic impact on the relationships that you have with your clients and on their ability to make progress.

PIT STOP

To have a clearer understanding of psychology and human behaviour, I suggest you read, a lot! In the resources section and on my website (which I link to at the end of the book), I have an extensive reading list for you.

As well as reading, I also suggest that you attend Dr John Demartini's Breakthrough Experience course. This is something that I did later into my career, and it would have been incredibly valuable if I had done it earlier. A large part of the two-day event was spent understanding perceptions (how we view ourselves, others and situations) and emotions.[9] Your current behaviour (often not complementary to your goals) is likely a result of tangled emotions, and it's the same for your clients. While at the event, I discovered that I had areas of my life that were limiting my ability to create a bigger vision. Using Dr Demartini's methods, I was able to realign my emotions and clarify my thinking. Any time you create clarity in your life, you will notice dramatic positive changes. Your clients are often pulled pillar to post with their emotions, which is why you see so much up and down throughout the coaching process. What I've covered in this section is at the route of many of your clients' struggles.

---

9   John Demartini, The Breakthrough Experience, https://drdemartini.com/breakthrough-experience, accessed May 2020

A clearer understanding of psychology and human behaviour will completely transform your coaching skills and ultimately your level of results.

Nutrition

Nutrition is an area that many coaches overlook. Our goal as coaches is to help our clients to improve their health, physical appearance, daily performance and, ultimately, their quality of life. To achieve this, monitoring the daily nutrition of our clients is key. It doesn't matter if you're new to the industry or you class yourself as experienced; you have the ability to improve, but without someone highlighting where you could be going wrong or stagnating, you'll end up doing the same thing every day and wondering why you're not getting results.

The first thing to appreciate is that each of your clients are different. They each have different goals, they live different lives, they have different levels of education around food, and they're all different shapes and sizes. So, the one-size-fits-all approach to nutrition never works. You might be using this approach and noticing that – as discussed in the 'Psychology' section regarding clients' behaviour – for some clients it works and for others it doesn't. This means that as coaches you need to go deeper into the nutritional needs of your clients. You need to know more about their relationships with food, current and past. You need to know more about their current lifestyles and professions. You also need to know how much your clients understand about nutrition. These pieces of information will enable you to create an appropriate starting place for your clients, and you'll understand how much support they'll need from you throughout the coaching process. Make sure you add questions about these topics in the questionnaires that you send out ahead of your consultations.

I often look back over the education that I was provided with when I qualified as a personal trainer, to remind myself what level of education fitness professionals are entering the industry with. Macro and micro nutrition was covered at a basic level – the basics of calories and the importance of nutrition for health (such as cardiovascular health) – but there was nothing that prepared me for the variety of clients that I was going to be working with. I learned nothing relating to behaviour and lifestyle, activity levels, experience, individual body shapes, body fat levels, muscle tissue, and how they all impact nutritional requirements. If you haven't studied nutrition in detail since you qualified, you are going to be at a big disadvantage when it comes to helping your clients to achieve results.

The first light-bulb moment for me surrounding nutrition came when I sat down with an early personal training mentor to discuss some of my clients and their levels of progress. I remember showing him a document of nutrition guidelines that I shared with all of my clients when I started working with them. I had listed out all the options for proteins, fats, carbohydrates and vegetables. I also had a meal plan template that my clients were supposed to follow every day. His first question to me was, 'What are you going to do for your clients if it doesn't work?' to which I replied, 'I don't know.' As he expected, I had some clients who were doing well and some who just couldn't seem to progress with this plan.

Now, you might be more experienced reading this and thinking that you know this already, but there are a lot of coaches out there who are following the one-size-fits-all approach and struggling just like I did. I hadn't considered how different each of my clients were, what their starting points were and even whether they were able to follow my guidelines. This one discussion completely changed the way that I looked at every client, and I hope that sharing it does the same for you. Question your knowledge of each area – client behaviour, lifestyle, body fat levels, muscle tissue – and how they all impact nutritional requirements. If you don't feel that you know enough, now is the time to Level Up your nutrition and start investing in your education.

The topic of clients' nutritional individuality leads nicely into a discussion of calories. After I moved away from providing general guidelines to my clients, I started researching calorie requirements a lot more. At the time, I wasn't working with any physique athletes, but I wanted to offer more specific nutrition plans for my clients. Providing a set number of calories to consume every day seemed like the perfect progression. I wasn't getting results with all of my clients by providing nutritional guidelines, so I thought, 'Surely they'd all get better results if I spelled out exactly how much of everything to eat.' Again, for some clients this would work, and for others it would lead to more compliancy issues. A lot of my clients would tell me that they simply couldn't eat the quantity of food that I was suggesting for them. I'm sure you've run into this issue, too.

At this point, I was questioning everything that I was doing, and if I'm honest I was getting more confused as the months went by. Over the years that followed, I tried everything – low carb, high carb, high protein, calorie cycling, macro plans. As I researched more and more, it seemed like every book that I read claimed to have the magic formula when it came to nutrition. I was relentless with my study simply because I had the goal of being well known for my coaching results, so I wanted to achieve results with everyone that I worked with. I knew that my reputation wasn't going to develop if I was only getting the odd result here and there.

Then, in 2009, I was introduced to Precision Nutrition, a course created by John Berardi.[10] It not only taught me about biochemistry (the chemical processes that

---

10   John Berardi, Precision Nutrition Certification, Level 1 (2009)

occur inside the human body), which I found fascinating, it also gave me a road map for working with all types of clients. As each area of nutrition was discussed, case studies were referenced alongside them. As I went through each section, I started to link what I was learning to the clients that I had been working with. The clients whom I was struggling to achieve results with on a structured and detailed calorie plan needed to be following basic guidelines with minimal adjustment. They were new to nutrition and exercise, so their nutrition needed to be reflective of their level of experience. Then, there were my clients who were quite experienced and who wanted to gain more muscle and develop a better body shape. I had been too vague with their nutrition requirements. They needed to be following more detailed nutrition programming, with set calorie plans, regular adjustments and much more thorough tracking.

As I continued with the course, I applied what I learned to each of the clients that I was working with at the time. I revised every single nutritional strategy and made sure that each client was following a protocol that was appropriate for their goal, their experience level and their lifestyle. From this, I created a new consultation road map, which I used when I signed up new clients. This helped me to work out exactly which strategy I was going to use with each one. To this day, we use this road map when we teach the M10 Matrix at our education seminars and mentoring programmes. As a coach, you need to be able to evaluate the questionnaires that your clients complete at the start of their journey and come up with the most appropriate strategy for them to follow. I always tell coaches that where you start the coaching process is just as, if not more, important than the months that follow. If you can achieve results with your clients in the first four weeks, you will have immediate buy-in from them. If your client starts to question your knowledge or your ability to help them achieve results in the early days, it's hard to regain control of the coaching relationship.

Nutritional programming is one of the most crucial skills that you can develop as a coach. Unlike nutrition more broadly, with nutritional programming you are looking deeper into the individual aspects such as micro nutrition (vitamins and minerals). All of the finer aspects can be adjusted as your clients progress through the coaching process, but the priority for the majority of your clients is going to be body composition. One of the first stages, therefore, is to create a nutritional programme that supports energy balance (the relationship between energy in and energy out).

One of the most common questions that the team at M10 and I get asked every week is, 'What diet do you think my client should be following to achieve X result?' Hopefully reading this section will clarify why the answer is often, 'It all depends'. There are many factors that you have to consider when you create any type of programming for your client, be that exercise or nutrition. Your job as a coach is to collect all of the information from your clients at the start of the coaching process (from questionnaires and speaking to your client) and decide which is the most appropriate starting place for them.

One of the most valuable things you can do as a coach is to sit down with a skilled and more experienced coach and go through each of your client case studies with them. There is no book that can tell you what to do with each client – that only comes with experience – but you can save yourself a lot of time by asking someone who has been in the same position that you are now in to help you. Make sure, however, that you ask someone who is currently working or has worked with the type of clients that you are working with. If you speak to a physique coach who is used to working with bodybuilders and body transformation clients, often they'll suggest a calorie-focused plan. There is nothing wrong with this approach for their clients, because the majority of them have short time frames to work with and their clients are more disciplined and likely to be more experienced. If you have clients who are quite new to exercise, the appropriate approach for them might be as simple as general guidelines.

Trust me, I have got it wrong many times. When I started to get into bodybuilding, I thought that all of my clients should be on the same style of plan as me and preparing six meals per day. As you'd expect, a handful of my clients did well following what I was doing (the more muscular clients), and the remainder couldn't stick to it at all. After scratching my head, I moved them onto a more appropriate strategy.

PIT STOP

Throughout your career, you will come across all body types, experience levels and goals, which is why it's important to understand the needs of your clients before you start to programme anything for them.

If you want to achieve results for all of your clients, take some time to review each of their case studies at the start of each week, and ask yourself if the strategy that you created for them is appropriate for where they are right now. Alongside studying the subjects that I have covered in this section, reach out to experienced coaches and review each of your clients with them. Allowing yourself to be vulnerable as a coach is one of the best things that you can do.

At the end of many of the courses that I attended, I would pay the lecturer to go through some of my clients' case studies with me. This helped me to fast track my results. Milos Sarcev was kind enough to help me with many of my clients. This was in my early days of working with physique athletes, and I wasn't skilled at manipulating calories when bringing someone's body fat levels right down. If it wasn't for his advice at the time, I wouldn't have pushed my clients to where they needed to get to. This set a new standard for what I could help my clients achieve, and it played a big part in helping me develop my reputation.

Hormones

For many of you, this book will be your first introduction to the subject of hormones. Some of you may have heard plenty about hormones, but you won't have considered the role that they play in helping you to achieve results with your clients.

Before I continue, it's important to remind you that you are not a doctor, so at no time are you qualified to diagnose or treat your clients. Why am I covering it, then? Well, as with the other areas of fitness that I have discussed so far in this book, a skilled coach is someone who has developed a coaching eye, which means that you are able to see things that the average coach can't. Your clients are communicating with you every day, and there could be a multitude of things preventing them from achieving results. In a lot of cases, you will just keep doing the same thing over and over, hoping that your clients will change, but simply having a deeper understanding of how the body works will enable you to adjust areas of your client's nutrition and training to facilitate their progress. Also, if you run into a wall and don't know what to do, a deeper understanding of your clients will allow you to decide if it's appropriate to refer out to a specialist (in most cases, it will be). *The more you know, the higher the level of service that you can provide for your clients.* The human body is complex; as such, in a lot of cases providing a nutrition plan and training programme isn't enough.

Hormones are chemical messengers that travel throughout the body delivering instructions to perform certain actions. They are responsible for controlling functions such as hunger, fullness, heart function, sleep quality, cell growth, sex drive, energy and the transportation of nutrients into cells. Here is a small list of hormones that you might be familiar with (there are around fifty hormones in total): thyroid hormones, insulin, oestrogen, progesterone, testosterone, cortisol, adrenaline and growth hormone. For optimal health and performance, we are ideally looking for our hormones to be balanced; however, this is rarely the case. Hormonal imbalances often occur when there is too little or too much of certain hormones circulating within the bloodstream. The side effects of imbalanced hormones can impact sleep quality, mood, energy, metabolism, sexual health, body composition, stress and other areas of life. I refer to these imbalances as 'red flags', and I'm sure they sound familiar to you.

There are many reasons why hormones could be out of balance, such as: medical conditions (diabetes, under/ overactive thyroid, autoimmune disease); high levels of stress; hormonal birth control; high levels of body fat; and a poor-quality diet. There is often a lot more going on with your clients than you might assume at first glance. It's common for certain symptoms that your clients are experiencing to be addressed when they take control of their lifestyles, health, exercise and nutrition; however, in certain cases you do need the support of medical professionals.

I'm not going to teach you about each of these areas in depth – that is where your own research and continued education comes in. My goal is to raise your awareness so that you can start to see your clients differently, ask more questions, listen more intently and then go in search of the answers.

To give you a better understanding of hormones and how they can impact your clients, let me share an example of a common type of client with you: a mum of two young children who are one and two years old. She has been trying to get back into exercise and lose some excess weight, but she's absolutely exhausted all the time. She says that she's tried to exercise on her own, but she can't get motivated to do it, so she hires you to help her get back in shape and feel better in herself. At her consultation, you find out that for the last two years she's hardly slept, and that she's been feeling very low emotionally. It takes her until midday every day to feel like she has enough energy to take on the day. She had very little appetite, so she's only been having some soup at lunch time and then a small sandwich in the evening.

When you sit down to plan out her nutrition and training, you have the goal of helping her to increase her energy, lose her excess weight and feel better, so you write out her diet, rich in healthy and nutritious food, you plan in three meals per day, and you create a gym-based training programme for her to follow three times a week. You provide your client with her nutrition plan and get started with her training. At the end of week one, your client tells you that she can't cope with all the food, she's even more exhausted than when she started, and she is going to have to reconsider her options. Because of your lack of understanding around hormones and stress, you wouldn't have linked everything that she was saying to you at her consultation.

Remember, she highlighted that she had zero appetite, she hardly slept for a year, and that she was very emotional. Armed with these red flags, the better option would have been to take your time, to listen more when she told you what she could do and ease her in slowly. It would have been a great idea to learn more about her lifestyle and sleep patterns, and to help her develop some new habits. It's likely that, her emotional state will come from being exhausted and not sleeping, so addressing sleep and lifestyle would have been a valuable first step for her. As soon as she starts to sleep more, she will have more energy; this will lead to an increased appetite, which will mean that she won't be so exhausted when she exercises. While this might be a slightly longer road to take, you will end up building a stronger relationship with your client, she'll stay with you a lot longer, and it's a lot likelier that she'll achieve results.

Everything that I've explained above is lifestyle advice, and I was able to give it because I had a deeper understanding of hormones and how they impact our day-to-day function. I did not treat or diagnose any symptoms, but – just like with nutrition – when you have a deeper understanding of your clients you are able to adopt a more tailored approach to creating their programming.

Here's another example of how hormonal imbalances can affect body composition – this time, in muscle building. Back in 2008, I was at the start of my competitive bodybuilding journey, and I was doing all I could to add more muscle to my frame. I was slowly increasing my calories and training as hard as I could. No matter what I did, my strength wasn't going up, my weight wasn't moving (but I was gaining body fat), and I was exhausted after every training session. I had just completed Biosignature Level 1 with Charles Poliquin. Biosignature was a system that was created around hormones; it taught me the link between optimal body composition, health and hormones.[11] A light-bulb moment for me was discovering that the quality of sleep and the strength of the immune system were linked to our ability to build muscle,

11   Charles Poliquin, Biosignature Level 1, www.poliquingroupeducation. com/biosignature-modulation.html

and that the health of the digestive system was also linked to the immune system and our ability to build muscle. In the months that followed, I continued my research into the immune system, sleep and digestion, and I was advised to work with a functional medicine doctor.

The functional medicine doctor recommended that I performed a stool test to see if anything was going on internally. The results showed that I had a pretty nasty parasite (*blastocystis hominis*, in case you wanted to know). The parasite was not only compromising my immune system, it was impacting my ability to digest protein. My weakened immune system was also making me tired all the time, and this is why I struggled to recover from training. This was not an optimal position to be in for muscle building.

Over the next twelve weeks, I followed a protocol from the doctor. After week six, I started to feel amazing, my energy started to increase, and I was sleeping much better. What was even more impressive was that at the eight-week stage I had gained 4 kg. I wanted to share this case study of myself to show that training harder and eating more for muscle gain might be the answer, in a lot of cases it will be but not always. Sometimes you have to listen more and learn to observe more, as there could be other things that you overlooked. After learning from Charles Poliquin, I went back over many of my client case studies and I was able to see so much more. Armed with the insight that I have shared in this section, you now have the opportunity to Level Up your understanding of hormones. You can learn more, which will help you to see more, which will help more of your clients to progress.

I'm sure you're wondering whether I have any recommendations for sources you can learn from. After my introduction to hormones from Charles Poliquin, I travelled to learn from the IFM. They have a course called the AFMCP (Applying Functional Medicine in Clinical Practice). If you do attend it, you'll be learning alongside doctors and healthcare practitioners. You will have to travel to attend the course, but I found it an incredible educational experience. Alongside the AFMCP, I highly recommend the work of Dr Bryan Walsh. He has an incredible teaching style, and a lot of his education can be obtained online (but if you get the opportunity to see him speak in person, you must). The online course of his that I recommend for every fitness professional is called Fat is Not Your Fault.[12] In it, Dr Walsh looks deep into the endocrine system and hormones and explains their relationship to body composition and health. He also shares many valuable strategies that you can use to support your clients with their goals.

I wanted to round up the Physical part of *Level Up* with a topic that I feel is incredibly important. There is something that really does separate the best from the rest:

---

12   Bryan Walsh, Fat is Not Your Client's Fault, fatisnotyourfault.com, accessed 14 May 2020

Are you ready to act every day with the intention of being the best coach that you could possibly be? Let me explain.

Purposeful coaching

In previous sections, I have covered the commitment that you are making to your own training, hiring your own coach, developing a coaching eye and committing yourself to your education. The only way you can truly Level Up the results that you achieve with your clients, your business and, ultimately, your career is by taking committed action each and every day. At every point in this book, I have provided you with challenging questions in the hope that you'll recognise the importance of progress, the importance of challenge, and the importance of having a clear vision of where you want to get to with your business and your life.

There are some people who will always get to certain points in their career and complain that they're not where they want to be. They will look to blame others, and they refuse to take accountability for their lack of progress. Then, there are others who wake up every day with the intention of making progress at every opportunity. They know that their level of success is ultimately down to the sum of their actions.

I'm sure you can think of someone you've observed professionally over the last few years who has progressed at a fast pace – someone who has produced result after result with their clients – and you can see their business and reputation growing week after week. I bet you've asked yourself time and again, 'What are they doing that I'm not?'

These are professionals who apply a principle that I call purposeful coaching. A purposeful coach coaches with the intention of achieving results with every single one of their clients. They are performing their coaching with the intention of developing a reputation for their craft. It doesn't matter who their clients are, what struggles they're facing, how complex their goal or how new they are to the coaching process – every part of the delivery of their coaching is centred around progress.

The word 'purpose' means 'with a sense of determination'.[13] A purposeful coach is determined to succeed for themselves and for their clients. Often the reason why your clients aren't making progress is because you're not acting out every part of your day and week with purpose, with the intention of progressing every part of your fitness business. If you applied everything that I have covered in this book so far, just think how much further you would be in your career and how much better your clients would be doing.

Remember: this book isn't about standing still, it's about Levelling Up, and *to achieve the level of progress*

---

13 Collins online dictionary, www.collinsdictionary.com/dictionary/
    english/purpose, accessed May 2020

*that I know you want, you have to act out every day with
purpose.*

My whole career has been purposeful, and that's
linked to the vision that I created at the start of my
career – the one in which I wanted to have a reputation in the fitness industry. I knew that to get there I
had to commit to a lot of education, coach at the highest level at all times, and act out every day like I was
heading in that direction. To get to where you want to
be, you're going to have to do the same. I know what
it's like to have your first client at 5.30am and finish
at 10pm; I did it for over fifteen years. I know what
it's like to feel tired at certain points of the day. But
if you have somewhere that you want to get to, this
is what it takes. You have to check in with yourself
at every part of each day and ask yourself if you're
delivering a high enough level of coaching. Has anything changed between your first session and your
fifth? Is there anything that you can do to step your
game up? If you are working with online clients, have
you started to get lazy with your check ins and could
you be delivering a higher level of service for your
clients? A coach who is acting with purpose will have
developed an internal check-in system. If you start to
feel lost at any stage of your career, this is often where
your motivation will waver, your standards will start
to slip, and you'll feel the energy that you're putting
into your coaching slowing down. You've lost your
sense of direction, and this can have a negative impact
on your business and your career. This is why I place

such a strong focus on the Personal sections of *Level Up*; you have to keep checking in with yourself if you want to keep progressing.

When you go back over the 'Creating a clear vision' section in the Personal part of this book, look at every part of your day from now on. Are you acting with purpose? Do your daily actions, your level of effort and the level of detail that you put into coaching each of your clients match the vision that you have for yourself and for your business? In the majority of cases, when you check back in with yourself and realign yourself with your vision and mission, you'll find a whole new level of energy. It's only at this point that you will be able to deliver a high level of purposeful coaching.

360 degrees of excellence to Learn More!

Take time right now to do a 360 degrees of excellence check in. Ask yourself:

1. Am I growing as a person?
2. Am I developing a better reputation?
3. Are my results where I want them to be?
4. Is my business growing?

This is your opportunity to start creating an action plan for your education, your physical development and the progression of your coaching. From this part of the book, what areas have you identified that need the most work? Create a list and get ready to start taking action.

In the Physical sections of this book, I have covered anatomy and physiology, biomechanics, psychology and human behaviour, nutrition, and hormones. These are five areas that I see as crucial for any coach when it comes to developing your education and progressing your career. I could have gone into more detail about weight-loss principles, body building, strength training or cardiovascular fitness, but these are more specialist areas. Some coaches focus on what they're passionate about (such as bodybuilding) and don't study the areas that will help all their clients. As a coach, you need to understand anatomy and biomechanics, as you're working with the human body and delivering exercise programming. You need to understand psychology and human behaviour, because you will be faced with different types of people who each present you with unique challenges. Lastly, nutrition and hormones support our ability to function optimally, whatever the results that you're trying to achieve. Each of these areas carry over to more specialist subjects, but I believe that they should be the foundation road map for any coach.

I hope you are starting to see the value of *Level Up*. Throughout your career, I want you to be able to come back to specific sections within this book and see if you're missing anything in your business or your life. This is a road map for you to follow – one that will help you to achieve your career goals.

PART THREE
Professional – Do More!

If there is one area that few fitness professionals are fully up to speed on, it's the professional side of running a fitness business. In fact, it's the one area that won't have been covered when you qualified. If you haven't had any previous experience in business, it's doubtful that you will have fully developed a business brain. Like the majority of fitness professionals, you'll be focused on learning and developing your coaching skills (which are essential), but you won't have your eyes on the operational sides of running and growing your business.

I spent quite a few years working in the property industry before I started my journey in the fitness industry. There were endless systems in place for each department that I worked in and a level of professionalism that had to be displayed both when meeting people and when communicating through letters (as it was back then) and email. There was also a lot of record keeping and data collection for measuring the company's performance. It was clear from the start that these were not only property industry standards – they were essential if the business was going to run smoothly and keep growing. My father always described my time in the property industry as the university of life. I was thrown in right at the deep end and I had to Level Up pretty quickly if I was going to survive.

When I started my career in the fitness industry, I immediately carried over many of the foundational skills that I had learned into running my business. I would set goals every month and record my progress, I created structured systems, and I would ensure that I communicated professionally with my clients on every level, both face to face and through email. It was clear to me early on that I was running my coaching business differently to the other coaches. My time in the property world had been valuable (though I didn't appreciate it at the time); as opposed to simply training my clients, I went straight into running a business. It wasn't perfect by any means, but I had a road map to start working from.

During my time in the property industry, I developed the foundations of a business brain. As I progressed in the fitness industry, I could clearly see who had what I call a fitness brain and who had a fitness business brain. Someone with a fitness brain focuses their efforts only on the coaching side, their knowledge and their own training. The coach with a fitness business brain focuses on their coaching, their knowledge, their training, and also the development of their reputation and business (which includes the quality and quantity of their results). This is a shift that will completely Level Up your development within the fitness industry and your life.

Professionalism

If you want to grow a successful business, it's essential that you develop a high level of professionalism. This means learning how to display the qualities of a professional and conduct yourself in a certain manner. If you have not worked in professional environments, you won't understand what levels of professionalism are expected of you. You also may not understand how important professionalism is when it comes to progressing your reputation, growing your business and increasing your income. You will find it difficult to charge more or increase your products and services as your career develops if you aren't operating with a high degree of professionalism.

Do you have a set of professional standards – a set of rules that govern how you run your business? These are very much like the personal standards that I shared with you in the Personal part of the book (you should have your own written down); like personal standards, I consider professional standards non-negotiables. Your personal standards are the commitments that you are making to yourself, and your professional standards are the commitments that you are making to your business and to your clients. If you've never seriously looked into professionalism before, it's doubtful that you'll know where to start.

Here are some key areas for you to consider:

- What level will you deliver your coaching at?
- What can customers expect when they work with you?
- What commitment will you make to your education?
- What level of results are you committed to achieving?
- What commitment are you making to your timekeeping?
- What commitment are you making to your personal presentation?
- How will you engage with your colleagues?
- How fast will you take action on your goals?

It's important that you now take some time and reflect on your current professional standards. Even though you might not have taken time to think about them recently, you will be operating with subconscious standards. This means that you're doing things every day without being aware that you're doing them. You might be slow in replying to your clients, you might be late for your clients or you might know that you haven't been committing to your education. You're only going to reach the new business vision that you have created for yourself if your professional standards match those of your vision. The subconscious standards that I have just mentioned certainly won't help you to reach your goals.

I had developed some valuable business skills when I worked for my dad and for other companies in the property industry, but I had to layer on a whole new level of professional standards to complement the reputation that I wanted to create for myself in the fitness industry. As my career developed, I would watch coaches who were more experienced than me, and I would pay close attention to how they delivered their sessions, the level of detail that they went into and how they would communicate with their clients. When I hired my own coaches, I would look through the programmes that they would write for me, and I would take note of the differences between their levels of communication on a weekly basis. I even did something similar when I would visit hotels and restaurants. There were always clear differences in levels of professionalism and customer service.

With each level of professional service that I experienced I would ask myself if there were particular professional standards that I valued. When there were, I would add them to my own list. I'm still extremely aware of professional standards and customer service, as they play an essential role in how a person and their brand are perceived.

PIT STOP

Turn your list of professional standards into a letter for yourself; this is called your professional promises letter. It's all very well having lists of action points, but what holds you accountable and creates a deep emotional connection that makes you follow through with them? I speak to a lot of coaches who have lists for everything, but they don't do anything with them. Create your professional promises letter and read it out loud to yourself at least once per week.

I'm sure you're thinking that this is a little strange but trust me – it's extremely valuable. The letter acts like a code of best practice for you and your business, and it will hold you accountable to your new professional standards. The letter starts with the words, 'I promise to'. Then you make solid commitments to yourself to deliver your coaching, run your business and achieve your goals according to your professional standards.

Here's an example of a professional promises letter:

I promise to sit down at the start of each week and review my professional standards. When I have allowed my standards to slip, I will address each one prior to progressing with my week. I commit to surrounding myself with driven people and always striving to better myself. I commit to avoiding distractions by remaining focused on my professional standards, and I will create a daily list of priorities that are linked to the areas that I value most in my life. I promise that all of my clients will receive an attentive, professional and positive experience when they work with me. I promise to regularly question myself, and I will commit to my education and apply everything that I learn. I understand that education is essential to me achieving high-quality results, which will support the development of my reputation. I commit to taking action on all of my goals, because I acknowledge that I will not progress my business and achieve my vision of owning my own gym by [year] if I do not take all of the necessary action. I commit to reading this letter to my loved ones and two colleagues that I respect in the industry. This is my commitment to be the best coach and professional that I can possibly be.

Can you see how powerful this type of letter is, especially if you read it to those who are closest to you? I'd like to think that you keep your promises, which is why letters like this carry so much more power than standard lists.

Reverse engineering

If you want to grow your business, your reputation and ultimately your income, you must have a strategy of how you're going to get there. It's all well and good having a vision, but the only way you're going to achieve it is if you break it down into actionable steps. Often, you'll get overwhelmed because you create an inspiring vision and then panic because you have no idea how you're going to realise it. Creating your vision is the first part; how you get there is where reverse engineering comes in. If your vision is five years in the future, you firstly have to break it down into yearly goals, and then into monthly goals. After you have your monthly goals written down, you need to work backwards to create weekly and then daily goals. It's the same if you can only see one year away (in the early stages of personal development, seeing five years ahead can be quite hard) – break down the year into monthly and then weekly goals. One of the main advantages of using this process is that you will be able to create a vision map. I create a document where I can see my big vision clearly, and then I set out all of the action steps that I have to take if I want to get there. A fitness business professional will start every week with goals. They're not winging it; everything has a reason and an outcome.

As you're starting to notice, developing yourself professionally is all about strategy. Think about how you help your clients to achieve their results. You break down their main goals into small manageable tasks. If they tick every box each week, it's likely that they'll reach their goals. You do this with your clients every week, but do you do it for yourself?

If you skipped over the 'Creating a clear vision' section early on in the Personal part of the book, go back to it now and decide on the direction that you want to take your business in. Without your vision in front of you, all you'll be reading in this section is individual strategies, and you won't be able to relate to where each one could fit into your business.

Understand that vision planning doesn't just take five minutes; for most people, it should take hours – in some cases, days. It's likely that you won't have thought seriously about it before, so you're going to have to dig deep. It's important that you bring your emotionally connected answers to the surface. One of the best ways to know if you've got the right answers from your vision planning process is if you feel deeply inspired when you think about them. When I sit down and create my business and life vision every six and twelve months, I keep digging into my thoughts until I feel deeply excited; most of all, I keep going until I can see my vision as if it was right in front of me. Your vision has the highest chance of becoming reality when you can see it. It's important to understand that your goals and tasks will change as you go through your career. Your vision will also change as you grow personally and professionally, which is why it's so important to revisit it every six months.

PIT STOP

Write out your reverse-engineered plan on a whiteboard in your home or at your office, or at the beginning of your journal (more on journaling later). You need to see it regularly, not only to remind you what you need to be doing but also so that you remain focused and inspired on your mission.

When you don't have a plan that you're working towards, you will find that you will get side-tracked and end up working on projects that have no relevance to your big vision. If you ever feel uninspired or demotivated, this is often the reason. When you don't have a vision, you will also compare yourself to other people. You will notice that your goals start to resemble those of the people who you are inspired by. While it's great having people that you're inspired by, you'll end up unfulfilled and uninspired when you're not working towards your own goals. Create your own vision, work back from each goal, create lists of monthly and daily tasks, and hold yourself accountable to completing each task. When you become disciplined with this format, you'll notice that your business will start to grow quicker than ever. Just like anything new, though, these habits take time to develop. How long is down to you and how you manage other distractions in your life.

Time management

Breaking down big visions into daily tasks leads nicely into time management, an area that the majority of fitness professionals struggle with. The first thing to understand is that we all have the same number of hours in each day; what you accomplish comes down to how you manage your time.

During my first ten years of owning M10, I coached over forty sessions of personal training each week, I worked up to coaching over fifty online clients, I opened the first M10 and then the second (there is only one now), and I wrote seven e-books, launched two websites, wrote over 250 articles, recorded over 150 educational videos, developed my physique, competed multiple times, managed and developed a team of five coaches at the first M10 and then six at the second, and I also started an education programme for fitness professionals (M10 Education). Not to mention, I travelled the world every few months to continue my own education.

There is no way that I would have been able to accomplish any of this if I wasn't disciplined with my time.

Every morning before I coached my clients, I would commit to writing part of an article that I was working on; I would do the same when I got home between 9.00pm and 10.30pm. I did that for years. I also trained at the same time every day and would never put clients in that time slot. At quieter times in the afternoon, I would manage the day-to-day running of the business, update clients' programming and create marketing content. I would also spend between forty-five minutes and one hour each day working on my education, reading or researching anything relating to my clients' case studies. On top of this, I would coach between six and seven clients per day, which would extend into Saturday and sometimes Sunday if necessary.

I'm sure you're asking when my social time was. I saw my friends and family on Saturday afternoons and Sundays; I had plenty of time. My reputation, the development of my knowledge, my physique and the growth of M10 were the areas that I had the highest value for. I was, and still am today, incredibly inspired by each of them. When you are inspired, you never struggle to make time. The things that you struggle with are often the areas that you're uninspired by. These are the things that you will always find yourself putting off, as you don't see value in them.

Prioritise

This goes back to linking your highest values, an area that I discussed in the Personal part of the book. You see, there will always be things that you think aren't important; these are the things that you avoid doing. I could have easily avoided writing articles, but if I didn't write articles, I wouldn't have any content to share. If I didn't have any content to share, how would anyone be able to learn from me? This would affect my ability to grow my reputation. I knew that the only times I would have to write articles would be before seeing my clients and when I got home at night, so those became their regular time slots. I hope you can see how I turned something that could have been low value into something that was high value. Think of all the things that you keep saying you'll do but keep putting off. Then, go back to the areas that you have identified as your highest values from the Personal part of the book.

I'm going to use research and education as another example, as this is a popular subject. Say that you know how important it is to continue to learn and attend courses, but you just keep putting it off. You schedule it in your diary but time and time again you allow other things to take precedence. You start to get frustrated because you want to do it, but you're just not making the time. There is a simple explanation: you just don't value research and education enough.

Now, let's do some linking. When you wrote out your values, you highlighted that your training, your clients and their results, and your relationship with your partner were the things that you had the highest value for. It's doubtful that you've taken the time to link research and education to your ability to act on each of your values. Your training would undoubtedly improve if you learned more, which would carry over to how much more you could help your clients. Your own training and progress would also give you more of a journey to share on your social media channels, which would help to develop your reputation. You would also develop a better coaching eye, which would enable you to see and explain more for your clients. Every opportunity for your clients to improve will increase their ability to achieve higher-quality results. More results mean more content, which means a better reputation, which also means that you will be able to charge more. If you're a personal trainer, your results mean more content online, which means that you could develop an online business as a secondary income stream. By growing your reputation and increasing your knowledge, it's likely that you'll see an increase in new clients and income; this improves the quality of your life with your partner. You are able to buy your dream house or car, and you're able to go on more holidays or plan more for your future. How does all of that sound?

Even though I have written this all out, linking should only take a matter of seconds. If we use the example above, in the future you should be able to look at the scheduled research and education in your diary and immediately link it to your training, results and the quality of life that you want with your partner. As soon as your emotion kicks in and you remind yourself how important each of your values are to you, you'll no longer struggle to make the time to study.

I'll be honest: when I first sat down to start writing this book, I questioned how I'd find the time to get it all done. But as soon as I thought about the areas that I valued, I immediately adjusted my day and tasks to create space first thing in the morning to get it done. Helping you all to grow and achieve fulfilling careers matters a great deal to me, and I had committed to you all that I would write the book. I also value my wife and the life that we are creating together as a family. If the business doesn't continue to grow, that will suffer. I hope you can see how they all link together, how your time management and values impact the areas that you prioritise in your life.

PIT STOP

Think about the things that you're doing every day that don't link to your highest values. These are the things that you can move to one side; they're not important. Now, think about the things that you're not making time for but that you acknowledge are important – can you link them to your highest values? You will see that by removing unimportant tasks from your day, you have created space for the things that you now value a lot higher.

If you apply these principles, you will have mastered one of the most valuable aspects of time management. When you are able to prioritise every part of your day, and you have a detailed action plan to follow (with each task inspiring you), you are truly unstoppable.

De-clutter your head

The next part of time management relates to clutter. The majority of fitness professionals that I coach walk around with everything in their heads, which results in a lot of chaos. The simple time management strategy that I teach them right at the beginning is to get their clutter out of their heads and onto paper or a whiteboard. When you can see your thoughts, your life will immediately become more structured. Let's have a look at some of the things that you're keeping in your head every day: your clients and all of their programming, your social media content, your training, food shopping, bills, income, and anyone who's contacted you that you need to reply to. The list goes on and on.

PIT STOP

At the start of every week, take everything that's in your head and write it down on a whiteboard (my personal favourite) or in a journal. Take a step back and look at it for a minute. Let's say you write down all of the names of your clients, then you write down which of your clients you still have to write programmes for. The latter become your priority for the next few days. The rest, you can leave on the board; you don't need to come back to them until next week. All of their programmes are now up to date, and they're progressing. This simple task has taken several clients out of your head and allowed you to prioritise the few programmes that need to be written. The new space that you have created in your head can now be filled with other priority tasks.

The same goes for your content. Every day, you're taking up vital space in your head trying to think of content. Often, you'll sit staring into space for hours wasting time. The simplest way to be more time efficient is to take all of your content ideas out of your head and write them on your whiteboard. Sit down at the start of each week, or even on Sunday, and plan out your content. What are your key topics for the week, what days are you going to post, are you going to use video or images, and how are you going to present your ideas? Create a grid on your whiteboard and fill it in. While this might take a little bit of time at the start of each week, all you need to do every morning is look at your whiteboard and you have your content set out in front of you. You're able to head into your day with headspace that you can fill with other priority tasks.

Using your whiteboard allows you to leave the house every day safe in the knowledge that you're only carrying current tasks and priorities in your head. You'll be able to think a lot clearer, and you'll also feel a bigger sense of accomplishment at the end of each day when your key tasks have been completed.

This brings us to journaling, which is something that I do religiously every day. Every night, I take everything that has accumulated in my head during the day and I write it on one page of my A4 notepad. One key thing that this does is support my ability to relax in the evening. Your rest and recovery are essential as a professional. All too often, you may lie awake at night thinking of all the things that you have or haven't done and then worry about whether you'll get everything done the next day. If everything is down on paper, you will find it easier to relax.

In the morning when I get up, I look at my whiteboard and see if there is anything that I need to move to a priority; I then create a schedule of action tasks for the day in my journal. I do a quick linking routine, which allows me to prioritise each task.

Remember: if you identify something as a priority, it will always get done.

By having all of my tasks down in front of me, I start each day with an action plan. I'm able to follow a schedule of tasks throughout the day as my journal determines the order. I will often get asked at this point if there is a strategy that I use for new tasks that come up throughout the day. Every day, new things will come up, and you have to make a note of them as they come in. Instead of being reactive and moving away from your scheduled tasks, you look at your list and ask yourself if the new tasks are more or less important than what you already have to do that day. This doesn't take long and allows you to be a lot more proactive. If the tasks don't require your immediate attention, they go to the bottom of the list, and they get added to your journal for review in the evening.

If you want to develop your business, build your reputation and increase your revenue, you have to be disciplined. Time management is all about structure – without it, you will always struggle to reach your goals. Just like any new skill, it takes time to learn, so don't just try it for a week and let it fall by the wayside. It has to become a part of you, something that you make a long-term commitment to. Once it's ingrained, you will notice how much clearer you feel, how much quicker you make decisions and how much faster you progress in all areas of your life.

Finally, it's important that you are just as structured in your personal life. Your downtime is just as important as your business schedule. Have a list of high and low priorities for social and leisure activities, and make sure that you are doing things that complement the areas that you value in life. It's easy to get drawn into things that other people want you to do; often these are things that they value. Stay in control of the direction that you want to go in, and always choose things that are complimentary to your goals. If social events with friends every weekend link to your values, then you'll be extremely fulfilled. If you are simply obliging others, you'll be unfulfilled.

Hats of a professional

One of the reasons why time management is so important is because there are so many parts to your profession. I'm going to touch on some of them in this section, not only so you can appreciate what a skilled professional is able to juggle on a day-to-day basis, but also to highlight areas that you might be overlooking or might need help with. A large percentage of businesses across all industries have many different departments, each of them specialising in different areas of business development. If you are a self-employed fitness professional, it's likely that you'll be covering all of them yourself – or at least trying to. As I mentioned earlier, if you haven't come from a business background there are going to be areas that you're not very skilled in.

To move your business forward, you can't just be a good coach; you are essentially switching between different professional hats all day. Here's are some of them:

- Customer service

- Operations

- Marketing and design

- Sales

- Accounting and finance

- Research and educational development

- Master of your coaching craft

When someone makes an enquiry into your business, you have to move straight into a *customer service* role. When you sign up a new client, you have to have all your systems in place to ensure a professional level of service. *Operations* ensures that you have all the necessary processes to be able to run an efficient and professional business. To attract and convert new clients, you have to spend a large percentage of your day on *marketing*. You'll have times of the day set aside to speak to prospective clients, either face to face, on the phone or by email, and you will need to switch into a *sales* mindset and focus on the growth of your client base. You can't grow your business if you don't understand money and you can't manage your *finances*. Many fitness professionals choose to sweep this area under the carpet, but your day must be driven by figures if you want to move forward, which means starting each day with targets. You will not develop your reputation and achieve results with your clients if you're not continually developing your *education*, so every day has to include time when you switch off your business head and focus purely on your professional knowledge. Finally, you have to be the professional who is delivering your *coaching*, be that face to face or online.

PIT STOP

Do you see now how many hats a fitness business professional needs to wear? How skilled are you in each area? How good are you at being able to switch between them every day? My guess is that you haven't given it a lot of thought.

Now, think about where your business would be if you were more skilled in each area – if you were disciplined and structured and had times set aside to focus on each area throughout the day.

Until you are able to delegate some of these roles (hiring more skilled professionals to work with you), you are going to have to learn how to do all of them, and you're also going to have to become skilled at time management. The key take-home from this section is the number of roles and responsibilities that you have, and how in control you have to be to run your fitness business. If you only focus on your coaching and ensuring that your clients are doing well, you are missing many of the other hats that are required to progress your business. You have many hats to wear. Some of them you've only just become aware of; others you know you need to wear but you don't fit them in. Go through each one and link them to your values; you'll soon adjust your way of thinking about them.

I start every day by writing in my journal (setting targets and writing in daily tasks) and writing articles (marketing). In between clients (professional craft), I would manage the team (operations), create content for the social media platforms (marketing), meet prospective clients for consultations (sales), and study (professional craft). I would also spend time being innovative and thinking of new ways that I could develop the business and increase income streams (such as online coaching, e-books and education). My day is scripted from start to finish.

I hope that by covering professionalism, reverse engineering, time management and professional hats, you're starting to see what you do as a profession and not just as training people. There is no excuse to be lazy, to waste time or to procrastinate. If you have a clear vision, if it inspires you, if you set out your goals each week and month, and if you have a task list, every day is going to be very busy. Not only that, but the thought of waking up every day should excite you.

Finances and money

Let me start this section off with some honesty. It took me a long time to value finances and money. At the start of my career, I just wanted to train my clients, train myself, learn more and focus on achieving results. Every part of my day in the early stages of my career was purely focused on fitness. I'm sure you can relate to this. Every week, I speak to coaches who struggle to tell me what they earn in detail and what their financial goals are.

At school, I did poorly with anything relating to maths and economics, and it was because I wasn't interested. In the Personal part of *Level Up*, I talked about growth and fixed mindsets. At school, I was fixed in my way of thinking around figures. If I'd had a growth mindset back then, I would have seen that I had the same opportunity as everyone else to do well in any subject, just as long as I applied myself. However, our ability to apply ourselves comes down to our ability to create a link, as we saw when we discussed values. I didn't see any value in learning about numbers and money, so I didn't apply myself. In this section, I want to help you understand the importance of finance and money and how it links to your values.

In the early days of my fitness career, I was hungry to fill my personal diary, simply to prove to myself that I could do it. I finally had a chance to prove to myself that I could succeed at something. I then began to realise that in order to achieve results with my clients, I needed to learn more. I remember the first time that I researched a course, my jaw dropped at the cost. It was the first time that I had considered spending so much of my money on something outside of my social life, clothes and holidays. I was committed to paying for it, but that was my first reality check that investing in myself was going to be key, but also costly. Coming from a property investment family and also having previous experience in business by then, it didn't take me long to connect the dots: if I earned more, I could study more. I didn't know it at the time, but I had created an immediate link between the results that I wanted to achieve with my clients and the level of education that I needed.

I was at LA Fitness at the time; if you wanted to charge more for your coaching, you had to attend courses from a set list. With my mind now focused on achieving better results and charging more, I started to book onto more courses. I will never forget the time that I came back from one course and I realised that I was now allowed to increase my hourly rate from £30 to £35. This one adjustment took my weekly income up by £150, which was £7200 over the year. I was now able to cover all of my education for the year ahead.

I was slowly grasping the concept that I was fully responsible for my future and achieving all of the goals that I had set for myself. I wanted to coach more clients, achieve high-quality results and develop my reputation. I was only going to achieve all of these if I learned more, travelled more and continued to increase my prices. There was also an important by-product of increasing my hourly rate: my confidence took a big step forward.

I started planning out my education calendar for the year ahead and setting aside income to cover each course. Many of them I paid for in advance so I could put the dates in my diary. This gave me a full year of education and travel to look forward to.

As my confidence grew, I started to create more challenges for myself. The next one came in the form of moving out and paying rent for the first time. This was a real turning point for me. I was paying rent at LA Fitness, I was saving money so I could study, and I was now paying rent for a room at my friend's house. For any of you reading this who are yet to move out of home, trust me, it's one of the best things you can do to develop a better relationship with money. Every day, I see lazy coaches who don't seem hungry to develop their businesses, and it's often down to not having enough responsibility in their lives. As soon as you have additional bills to pay, you will have a different level of appreciation for money, and you'll attack each day with a completely new level of urgency.

PIT STOP

Do you have moments when you just don't feel in control?

Now that I had more responsibilities, I didn't want to get lost, so I needed to take control and be more organised with my money. If I wanted to earn more, so I could study more, travel more, pay my rent and increase my reputation, I needed to manage my finances better. For the first time in my life, I was becoming interested in something that I completely avoided at school. I wanted to know more about money, saving it and earning more of it. I wasn't hungry to make money just for the sake of it; I was excited because I could link it to everything that I wanted to achieve.

If you believe you're bad with money, you're not – you simply don't value it. Either you haven't identified your values, or you haven't considered linking money and finances to the things that you value. Go back to your vision, perform the reverse engineering process, and you'll start seeing the important role that money plays in your ability to reach your goals. This will change your relationship with money.

A lot of fitness professionals think that money is a bad thing and associate it with being greedy. I'll be honest: in the early days, I did think like this. However, there is another way of looking at it. If you earn more, you will be able to learn more. When you learn more, you are able to help more people. You're in the industry to help people, to teach people how to live a healthier, fitter and happier life. With limited knowledge, you'll always struggle to achieve results with your clients and to communicate through your marketing channels (more on this later). If you can't reach people, you won't have a full diary. This limits the level of impact that you can make in people's lives. If you coach more people and help them to achieve their goals, you are paid more. This income can then be used to further your knowledge and to help even more people, but it also supports your ability to reach your personal goals. If your clients improve their health, fitness and relationships with their bodies, they will see many benefits in their lives, such as increased energy, improved self-confidence and greater happiness. You are helping people to achieve their dreams, while at the same time achieving your own. Always remember that *by paying you for what you do, your clients are receiving something a lot more valuable in return.*

My first step in learning more about money was to hire an accountant. I was responsible for recording the coaching sessions that I was doing, the income that I was bringing in, my outgoings and the receipts that I was giving out to my clients. Back then, I had a brown paper receipt book, and I provided all of my clients with a record of their payments. At the end of every month, I took my receipts and my diary to the accountants, and they sat down with me to cross-check everything. At the end of every quarter, they would draw up my quarterly accounts, they would talk me through any tax implications as the year progressed, and we would look at the months ahead so I could create some projections for my earnings.

Simply looking further ahead gave me the opportunity to work out if I was going to be able to afford all of the things that I wanted to do. If we identified that there were quieter times in the year ahead (such as Christmas), I would adjust my outgoings accordingly. If I told them that there were investments that I wanted to make into my education later in the year, they'd explain how much I'd need to save to afford them.

One thing that I had never fully appreciated before was gross and net income. I always used to add up the number of sessions that I was doing and multiply it by my hourly rate. This figure (gross) will always make you happy, because it doesn't take into consideration all of your bills and taxes. If you only focus on the gross figure, it's likely that you'll be spending way above your means every month. Your net income is the amount that's left once you have paid all your expenses. By sitting down with my accountant every month, I was forced to look at the reality of my business and make forecasts – estimates of future income and expenses for my business across a set period of time. I speak to a lot of fitness professionals who mentally live by the gross income and spend according to what they see coming in. Then panic sets in at the start of every month when they have to pay their rent and bills. It depends what country you are in, but the majority of you will have to pay taxes. By not creating a forecast of your outgoings every month, quarter and year, it's likely that you won't have saved enough money as the year has gone by, and you'll be faced with a hefty tax bill.

When I told my accountant that I wanted to start renting a room, he added the rent amount to my forecast in the Excel sheet and I saw an immediate drop in my net income. It was a reality that drove me to study more, which allowed me to increase my hourly rate so that the outgoing rent amount didn't impact my net income. This resonated with me because a drop in my net income meant that I would have less money to invest into my education, and not having the money to invest into my studies made me feel like I was standing still. A quick linking process got me back on the gym floor and achieving higher-quality results, which resulted in me being able to charge more. I might seem like a broken record, but can you see how I am always referring back to everything that I value? I was inspired to earn more, firstly because I could see on paper what I needed to bring in, but also because I had a clear vision of where I wanted to get to in my career.

Another aspect of finances that I want to bring to your attention is borrowing. In my early days, I didn't even consider the possibility of having a mortgage, and it never crossed my mind that I would own a gym. However, my father had many years of experience in this area as a property investor. He would always talk to me about the future. Sure, I had a vision of wanting to have a reputation in the fitness industry and achieve high-quality results, but I hadn't thought about investments or going beyond being a personal trainer in the health club. The conversations I had with my father about the future were always a challenge, as he wanted me to look deeper into my accounts, ensuring that they looked good in case I ever wanted to borrow money. I was so focused on spending my money on my education, I didn't want to look that far ahead. However, I listened and was always diligent with my accounting. I would bank all of my income, save for taxes, and continue to work with my accountants.

Several years later, my dad and I were discussing getting my first mortgage. He said that the bank would need to see my accounts. I remember looking up at him and smiling, and he knew exactly why. I said, 'It's a good job the accounts are all up to date and showing all of my income.' He reminded me of our earlier conversations and said there was no way that the mortgage application would have gone through without them. The same thing happened prior to opening M10 in Nottingham. This time, I wanted to borrow a large sum of money from the bank to get the gym started. I had to present the bank with the accounts for M10 Newark (my first gym), and they also had to see a business plan to showcase the vision that I had for the business.

I owe a lot to my father for the conversations that we had in the early days. You might not think that you'll need to borrow money in the future, but I guarantee you will. It might be for a mortgage, for a car, or even if you choose to open a gym/studio. You need to have your accounts in order – and the sooner you start, the better.

As well as having my finances in order, I would not have been able to borrow the money to start M10 in Nottingham without my additional income streams. The benefit of having a vision and forecasting is that you can see further into the future. You have a detailed plan in front of you, and you can see clearly whether your current level of income is going to help you to reach your goal. The reality for a lot of you reading this is that you'll get to the point in your career where you will want to borrow money or finance something big, and you'll see that your current income isn't enough. In hindsight, if you'd been following a financial plan for the years leading up to this point, you'd have put strategies in place to be earning more. I speak to many coaches who haven't increased their prices in years, yet they're frustrated that they can't afford to invest more in their business, move to a new house, go on more holidays, or even afford to live a more comfortable life. As I've said throughout this book, the level of progress that you make during your career is completely up to you. Without a vision and a plan, you are simply winging it, and if you approach your business and life like this, you'll struggle to see an increase in your income. If, on the other hand, you do plan, and you can see what you need to be earning one year, three years and five years from now, you can make all the necessary adjustments to ensure that you get there.

For the first four years of my career, the only additional income I made was from increasing my hourly rate. However, for every £5 that I increased, I received an extra £7,200 (gross) each year. I increased my hourly rate three times, which earned me an extra £21,600 in total. The majority of this additional income went straight back into my education, which helped me to increase my coaching results, which also supported my vision of increasing my reputation.

PIT STOP

If you knew that you could increase your income by £21,600 over the next three years, what would that help you to accomplish?

It's likely that you've never sat down and looked at your potential earnings. What if I said to you that you could earn another £21,600 by increasing your hourly rate over the next three years, and then you could add another £12,000–£18,000 by adding some online coaching (ten to fifteen online clients at £100 per month). You actually have the potential to earn an extra £39,500 (gross) over the next three years.

What could this extra income do in terms of the things that you value in your life and the vision that you have for yourself? If you value your knowledge and ability to achieve results, you could travel to learn from more people all around the world. If you value your family and financial security, you could afford to buy your dream home. I valued my clients, my knowledge and training; as such, every additional income stream that I created went straight back into building my dream gym and getting the best equipment. It also went back into my education so that I could teach my clients more, achieve better results and develop my team.

My reputation, knowledge and results have helped me to not only increase my hourly rate but also to develop internships for coaches (in the early days) and online coaching programmes, open gyms, create e-books and video courses, and launch seminars, mentorships and my business mastermind. They've also helped me to be in a position to do something that I never thought I'd ever do – write this book for you. Each of my income streams have been planned according to my vision, both personally and professionally, and also in line with my financial forecasts.

Income streams will play a vital role in your ability to earn more throughout your career; however, you won't be in a position to add them if you don't plan for them. If you're wondering what keeps people inspired and motivated, it's all the plans that they have for their future and the road map that they are following that will help them to get there.

Now, it's one thing me explaining about income, outgoings, taxes, borrowing, forecasts and income streams, but it's another thing getting you to apply them. As with everything that I have covered in *Level Up*, I want to help you to make progress. In order to be in control of your money, you need to see it. Sitting down with my accountant every month gave me a completely new appreciation for my finances, but, more than that, it gave me targets to work towards each week; it gave my day-to-day tasks a new meaning. I had a direct link between the number of new clients that I needed, the amount of coaching that I needed to do each week, the income that would bring in, and what it all meant in my overall vision for my career and for my life.

Please don't just read this section, acknowledge that finances and money are important, and then do nothing with them. Taking action is going to mean sitting down (preferably with an accountant) and working through a lot of numbers. It's likely to be uncomfortable, because it'll highlight how sloppy you've been with your figures up to now. One thing I can promise, though, is an immense sense of calm and structure when you have your accounts in order.

Branding

My first introduction to branding was just before I opened the first M10. I went to see a friend of mine called Keith who had offered to help me create the M10 logo. We sat down and, in all honesty, I thought we were just going to talk about fonts and colours. But the first thing he said was, 'Tell me about M10. What is it, who is going to be going there, what are people going to experience when they go there? What do you want people to say about M10?'

I hadn't given it a great deal of thought. I wanted to open a personal training facility for my clients, and that was my main focus. After some digging and more challenging questions, it became quite clear what I wanted to create: a private, professional facility where my clients experienced a high level of coaching and customer service. I wanted the facility to be smart, modern and clean. I wanted M10 to be regarded for the results that it helped its clients to achieve, and I wanted people to get a feeling of high value when they experienced coaching at M10. After listening to me, Keith highlighted that M10 was going to be an extension of what I had already created for myself. In my town, I was already known for my coaching results and for my level of service, and I had a waiting list of clients who wanted to work with me. Keith explained that I had spent the last four years developing my personal brand without even knowing it.

This was the first time that I had branding explained to me, and it was a breakthrough for me professionally. The majority of fitness professionals that I speak to see themselves as trainers or coaches; they don't see themselves as brands. If you own a gym or studio, it's likely that you'll see yourself providing a place for people to train under a company name, but you don't see your business as a brand. Until you understand that what you do is completely unique to you, you will always regard yourself as the same as everyone else.

I have spent every day since the M10 brand was created growing it alongside my personal brand. The details of how I have done that and how it has helped me are unique to me; however, if you've followed each section of this book so far, you'll understand the lengths that I've gone to in developing my reputation throughout my career. This section is all about you and how you can develop your own personal or business brand. This is your chance to create your own space within the fitness industry. Levelling up in all of the areas that I've covered will take you a long way towards growing your brand.

The fitness industry isn't a saturated market. I hear fitness professionals saying all the time that it's so hard to grow a business, but if this were true why are there so many successful people and businesses in the world across all industries. You only have to go to the famous Harley Street in London to see how many doctors and dentists there are on one road. How can so many professionals be located in such close proximity to each other and all be doing so well?

The answer is that they have all been able to differentiate themselves in their marketplaces; they have each built a reputation and many of them rely on word of mouth. They have become known for their levels of service and for their results. Because of their experience, customers feel compelled to not only keep coming back but also to keep telling their friends to come. I spoke to one dentist on Harley street in 2018, and she had not created one marketing campaign since she had been there. She had built her business on word of mouth alone. She told me that everyone in her business works to maintain the standards of the brand and ensures that every customer has an experience from the moment they call to the end of their treatment (which includes aftercare).

If you're struggling to grow your business, you just haven't found your way of standing out yet in the fitness industry. You haven't identified what differentiates you from other fitness professionals. When you develop a new set of eyes and start to see what you do as a brand, you will approach your marketing (more on this in the next section), your clients and their experience in a completely different way. *If you want to stand out, if you want to develop a reputation, if you want to charge more, and if you want to develop more products and services, branding is essential.*

Branding is an extensive topic and one which I urge you to study in more detail. In this section, I want to highlight some of the areas where I feel the fitness industry can improve, and, most importantly, areas that I know can yield growth if you master them.

Brand image

The first thing to consider when developing your brand (personal or business) is: what do you want people to say about you? Imagine your customers and their friends are having a coffee discussing your brand – what impression have you left in their minds? If people see your marketing, what do you want them to perceive about your brand? Everything you do and say leaves an impression on people, and if you want to position yourself or your business within the fitness industry and develop your reputation (which is key if you want to progress), you have to act every day as if that is your intention.

You are fully responsible for your brand image. If you don't want people to perceive you or your business the wrong way, take time to sit down and write out what 'the right way' would look like to you. Then, make every effort to deliver your service and your marketing consistently at all times.

Brand personality

Aligned closely to brand image is brand personality. This aspect of branding goes deeper than wanting to be perceived as professional and delivering high levels of customer service. It relates to the feeling that you want to give your customers. Do you want to be perceived as happy, humorous, caring, considerate, educated or influential (to name a few options)? When you consider your marketing and the relationships that you want to develop with your potential customers, understand that people like people who are like themselves. Some people will connect with your brand; others won't. It's important that you're ok with that. You need to showcase your brand personality when you present your brand to the marketplace.

Brand equity

Do you ever consider whether people perceive you as valuable? Think back to the last time that someone said 'no' to you. Why do you think that was? It wasn't because they didn't like you or the clothes you were wearing; it was simply because they didn't see the value in investing. Prior to investing in anything, we always have to see the value in it.

I don't know a fitness professional who doesn't want to earn more money or eventually have more than one income stream. So, what is the key to being able to charge more or add more products and services? You must be seen as premium – it's that simple. This is why I always tell coaches that there is always room to charge more. In the town that I started personal training in, within four years I was charging more than any trainer had ever charged. It was a small market town where the highest hourly rate was £30, and I was charging £50. Most people told me that it wasn't going to be possible, but I proved them wrong. I had achieved better results than anyone else, and I was featured in the local press, I held small talks every couple of months, I was in demand (in fact, I had a waiting list), and my clients all enjoyed working with me. These all supported the value that people perceived they were getting if they worked with me. Any person whose brand is perceived as high value and who has been able to charge a premium for their services has carefully created these circumstances.

Brand experience

One of the most important aspects of branding is the brand experience. It doesn't matter how knowledgeable you are, how you look or how hard you train; if your clients don't have a valuable experience with you and your brand, they won't stay with you, and they certainly won't recommend you to their friends.

The brand experience begins the first time someone has an interaction with your brand. It is the combination of all experiences and interactions that your customers have with your brand. For your customers to have a positive experience, your brand values and brand personality must be aligned and presented throughout the delivery of your service. A positive brand experience is the key to developing your customers trust.

People always remember how you make them feel, and they will also recommend experiences that exceed their expectations.

If the brand experience isn't aligned with your customers' expectations, you will always struggle to increase your reputation, your ability to add additional products and services to your brand, and your ability to increase your coaching fees.

PIT STOP

Take some time now to write down every aspect of your current brand experience and ask yourself if they're aligned with your brand values, brand image and brand personality, and if they're impacting your brand equity in the right way.

Brand extension

There may come a time in your career when you will want to add additional products and services to your brand. You've seen plenty of people who have done it, and I'm sure you've wondered why it looks so effortless for them. Brand extension refers to when a brand is able to leverage its reputation to introduce new products and services into the marketplace. The key word here is 'reputation'. The successful way to introduce new products and services is to ensure that your existing brand is already well known.

When you have successfully developed the first product in your brand, you will have built up your reputation and you will have a portfolio of quality results. You'll have a list of customers who have already purchased from you once, and in the majority of cases you will have used your reputation to develop a (local and/or social media) following. At this stage, you have earned the privilege called brand extension. Your audience will be asking you for more ways to work with you, or you have a larger audience that you know you can sell to but you don't have the products and services for them (yet).

Marketing

When I first sat down to create the road map for this section, I honestly panicked a little. Marketing is such a big topic, and I could write another book just on what I have learned about it throughout my career. But I asked myself whether there was an individual topic within marketing that's important for you to grasp – one which will give you the biggest opportunity to Level Up. The answer was not a single topic within marketing; it was the entire process.

If you ask most people what they think marketing is, they'll often say sales or promotion. They think it's the individual posts that people make on social media, videos or magazine articles. Most people think its individual components, when in fact it's so much more than that. Marketing is a process; it's all about building relationships.

I became fascinated by marketing when I first started asking people how they had heard about me. I realised that there were so many different ways that people were coming across me, and in a lot of cases it had taken them quite a long time to end up sitting in front of me. How was this happening, and how much control did I have over it? At first, I was just grateful that new clients were reaching out to me on a regular basis, and then I decided to delve deeper.

I could cover individual sections of marketing such as email, social media, local marketing and websites, but they all have one thing in common: they are all about developing relationships. If you can understand how you can get your audience's attention, keep them entertained and convert them into customers, you have the marketing formula. Without a clear understanding of this, all you're doing is throwing individual tactics around without any strategy.

I explain marketing to fitness professionals like it's a conveyor belt (marketers refer to it as a funnel). The first time someone hears about you, they hop onto the beginning of a moving conveyor belt. They are slowly being pulled along, but just like all conveyor belts there is an end. If you can hold your potential customer's attention for long enough, at the end they will be picked up by a crane, and they won't fall off the end. This is your new customer. If you fail to hold their attention, they'll fall off the end and it's likely that will be the last time you'll see them. Your job as a marketer is to do everything in your power while they're on the conveyor belt to turn them into a customer. The three main marketing stages are commonly referred to as awareness (start), consideration (midpoint), and conversion (end), and I like to add two more, retention and referral.

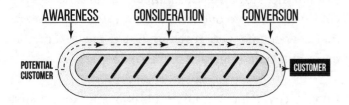

Awareness

Making people aware of you is all about attention. What are you actively doing to make people aware of your personal or business brand? In many cases, fitness professionals spend a lot of their time studying, training and coaching clients, but you're only able to do the work that you do because of new customers. I've discussed your role as a professional at length in this book, and delivering your craft is just one part of your job role. In order to have a consistent stream of new customers, you need to be developing new connections every single day. This means learning how to become a skilled marketer.

On average at M10, after someone finds out about us (awareness), it can take them two to three months to actually make contact and arrange to come into the gym for a consultation. This is the length of time that it takes us to develop a strong enough relationship that our potential customers feel that we're the right place for them. If we're only marketing every few weeks, we'll have a conveyor belt with only a few people joining at any one time. If I want the crane at the end of the conveyor belt to be picking up new clients for us at least a few times each week, new potential customers have to be joining at all times.

PIT STOP

Think back to the last time that a brand first caught your attention. Maybe someone told you about a brand and you searched for it online; you might have seen it on social media or even on TV. If you had any interest in the brand, did it make you stop and think? Did it leave an impression on you? This was your first engagement with the brand; this is when you first became aware that the brand exists.

When you first become aware of a brand, you might spend a little more time researching the brand and seeing if they have anything else that is of interest to you. It might be that you take no action at that point, but you make an effort to visit the brand again at a later time. This is where impressions really do count. Every single potential customer is searching for something; sometimes they know exactly what they want, and at other times they need to have it highlighted to them. This is what makes the awareness stage so important and interesting as a marketer. Has the first engagement with your brand made your potential customer want to come back? Has it made them want to delve deeper into what you offer and learn more about the information that you share? Maybe they'll choose to start following you and even engage with you.

Remember, marketing is all about building relationships. Think about the first time that you meet someone. Immediately, you ask yourself if this is someone that you think you'll like. You assess the first impressions immediately. Then, after talking for a while you ask yourself if you'd like to meet up with the person again. A large percentage of your decisions are based on the personality of the person and the value that you're getting from the conversation (whether you find them engaging). New friendships and relationships are all about marketing. If you enjoyed the first engagement, the relationship has the potential to move on. If you didn't, it doesn't go any further. Now I want you to think about your own marketing (relationship building). Think about yourself as a personal brand – how many new people do you speak to every day, and are you conscious of the impression that you are leaving them with? As a company brand, what are you doing every day to stop your potential customers in their tracks? How are you getting people's attention?

When people have found out about you and you've managed to get their attention, what are you doing to hold it? Great brands build relationships and they provide you with a stream of information that makes you want to engage at a deeper level. You keep wanting to come back for more. I'm sure you've experienced that yourself. You will always struggle to develop relationships and hold someone's attention if you're not providing them with information that they see as valuable, but in order to provide high value you need to know everything about your target customer.

When I create my marketing strategies aimed at fitness professionals, I have two pictures on my wall in my office. One is of a relatively new personal trainer who is standing with their arms folded in a commercial gym; the other is of a more experienced coach who is standing in their own facility. The first picture reminds me of the coaches that I am speaking to who are in the first one to five years of their careers, and the second picture reminds me of the more experienced and entrepreneurial coaches. For each type of coach, I have an extensive list of the areas that they struggle with on a day-to-day basis, what they need to learn more about and where I think they're heading in their career. If you've ever read any of my content, it's likely that you thought I was writing specifically for you. My goal when I create content is to get your attention, hold your attention and keep you coming back for more. I hope you can now see how important it is to know who you're speaking to. A lot of fitness professionals want to know which is the best style of marketing before they've identified their target audience. If you take this approach, you'll only end up getting the attention of the wrong audience. Prior to doing any marketing, make sure you've identified who your target audience is first.

Here are a few areas to consider:

- What is their age?

- What is their sex?

- What career do they have?

- What income bracket are they in?

- What are their goals (personally and professionally)?

- What do they struggle with the most on a day-to-day basis?

- What is stopping them from achieving their goals right now?

- What are their biggest fears in life?

The list goes on and on if you take some time to dive into the needs and desires of your target audience. The more you learn about them, the better you will become at marketing to them.

When you know who you are talking to, you can choose the most appropriate channels to reach them and hold their attention. This is where I could start writing a full book on the subject. You have to make yourself visible to your target audience.

Here are some examples of how you can introduce your target customer to your brand:

Personal trainers

- Flyers

- Seminars

- Speaking to local businesses

- Speaking to members of your gym

- Podcasts

- Websites

- Social media

Gym / studio owners

- Social media

- Websites

- Speaking to local businesses

- Paid advertising (such as Google and Facebook ads)

- Podcasts

Online coaches

- Social media

- Websites

- Podcasts

- Paid advertising (such as Google and Facebook ads)

Once someone has become aware of you, the next step is to hold their attention. This means that you have to provide ongoing valuable information for them that isn't focused on selling (not yet, anyway). In the early stages of marketing, it's important for people to like your brand, and that means helping them in as many ways as possible. If you follow me on a regular basis, you'll see how much content I give away for free – my podcast, social media content, live feeds, articles and even free products. Everything that I create is aimed at helping you as much as possible so that you learn to like and trust me.

PIT STOP

Think about all of the people that you follow on social media. Why is it that you keep going back to their content? It's because you're either learning something from them or you're being entertained in some way. If you're not choosing to unfollow them, they are providing you with value. They've done a great job of getting your attention, and now they're developing a relationship with you.

An example that you'll all resonate with is personal training on the gym floor. The first stage of awareness is simply getting someone's attention. This might be a wave at them across the floor. You're making them aware that you exist. Believe it or not, this is very powerful and engaging. Many fitness professionals don't realise that this is the first stage of relationship building.

The person who is prepared to strike up more conversations is the person who will always be ahead of the game when it comes to marketing and developing a community. When I was working on the gym floor in my first role as a personal trainer, I made it my job to know absolutely everyone in the gym. I said hello all the time, I knew everything about everyone, and – guess what? I had a waiting list quicker than anyone else there. You have the same opportunity as everyone else to Level Up your marketing and make yourself more visible to your target audience. If you develop this skill (which does take time to master), you will have created the foundations of your marketing road map.

Consideration

Now that you have a list of people who you are speaking to on a day-to-day basis, and you are developing relationships with them nicely, it's time to take it to another level. People may follow your content on social media, but that's all they will do if you don't move them forward. The consideration stage of the conveyor belt is all about commitment – can you take your target audience to a point where they show a deeper level of interest in your products or services?

Every day, you read articles, you consume content on social media, you listen to podcasts, and you speak to people face to face. For a lot of what you consume, you haven't considered investing in what the creator is offering. What you don't realise is that every piece of content that you take on board is creating a sublimi-nal message. A good marketer is delivering content that is highlighting all of the areas that you're strug-gling with (they know you). They are also informing you in all of the areas that you enjoy learning about, and you will be forming a deeper connection with every piece of content that is being shared. It's the same thing with face-to-face conversations. The more subjects they bring up that are linked to the areas that you're interested in, the more you want to speak to that person. Think about someone who you recently started engaging with – have they done a good job of building a relationship with you? Do you feel drawn to their content or look forward to every time you meet up with them?

At this stage, you won't be the only person who's trying to get the attention of your target audience. So, having a strategy in place to move them along the conveyor belt is key. In marketing, if you're always moving your target audience along you always have a chance of being ahead of your competitors.

The goal of the next step is to show your audience that you can solve their problem and to raise their level of urgency. Articles and conversations only go so far; it's now time to see if they're ready to take action. Have you ever taken a free trial for anything? I bet you've had a test drive in a car. You've followed your favourite model of car for some time, you've read all about it and saved loads of pictures, but you haven't done anything about it. Then, one day you see an article in a magazine offering a twenty-four-hour test drive, and they will even deliver the car to your doorstep. After months of consuming content (awareness), you see an offer that is irresistible. This is when you move into the consideration stage. All you have to do is call up the showroom, leave all of your contact details and give them the full spec of your dream car from that manufacturer, and it's all yours. Three days later, the car arrives at your home, and you spend the next twenty-four hours in complete luxury. When you have to give the car back, you're gutted; you absolutely loved it. However, you can't quite make your mind up, so you don't push forward to purchasing it (I'll come back to this part in the 'Conversion' section).

As another example, say you have been speaking to a potential client in the gym for a few weeks. Your conversations have progressed significantly. You know a lot about them, and you have a laugh when you see each other. You know that they have a holiday coming up in four months, and you know that they have been struggling with their diet. However, you also know that it's too early to propose your coaching services to them, so you move into the consideration stage of marketing. You know that their biggest issue is their diet, so you offer to write out the next fourteen days of their diet for free. They bite your hand off, they're extremely grateful and they promise to stick to it 100%. They know from speaking to you how knowledgeable you are, and they also know how much you can help them. But just like so many people, if they're going to even consider investing, they want to know that what you're offering works. Over the next fourteen days, they keep in touch with you, and the weight starts to fall off. You think you've got this in the bag, so after they've done their weigh-in you propose that they carry on with you and book some coaching sessions. You're a little bit baffled when they tell you that they'll think about it. As a marketer, you shouldn't be frustrated, though, as this is all a part of the process. This is not the end – far from it. I'm going to explain in the 'Conversion' section how it all comes together.

After the initial awareness stages, you need to give your target audience something that is as close as possible to the service that you offer. *You need to help them to achieve part of their solution, but not all of it.* Whatever you offer has to be linked closely to the problems that your audience are facing. The broader the offering, the less likely your audience will engage with it. To give you an example, fat-loss guides are seen as low value because people have something more specific in mind. Are they more focused on specific areas, such as seeing their abs? Is it male or female fat loss that you're targeting? The more specific you can be, the more your offering will resonate with your audience.

Below are some examples of offerings that you could use during the consideration stage:

Personal trainers

- Free small seminar or workshop (on a specific topic)
- Free thirty-minute training session (focusing on a specific area)
- Free fourteen-day training and nutrition plan (specific to their goal)

Gym / studio owners

- Free small seminar or workshop (targeting the primary goals of their members)
- Free seven-day trial to use the gym
- One free pass to try a class (specify which class)

Online coaches

- Free thirty-day weight-loss plan (aim to achieve a set goal in thirty days)
- Free body-part training plan
- Free guide to help them to lose their first 10 lbs

These examples are not guaranteed sales; they are part of the marketing process. In some cases, providing this level of value for free is enough to prompt someone to enquire into working with you or signing up for a membership at your gym. Experiencing a part of what you do was enough to tip them over the edge. In many cases, however, there is still plenty of work to be done.

As a marketer, your job is to keep in contact, be that through email (get as many of your prospective clients' email addresses as you can), consistent social media and website content, and developing your face-to-face conversations. As a marketer, you have to learn how to be persistent. You have to appreciate that for someone to end up investing in you, your products or your services, they have to perceive you as high value. Until then, do all you can to raise your level in their eyes.

Conversion

This is the stage when it all comes together – this is when you acquire your customer. The conversion stage is when they know that they have a problem, they know that you can solve it, and they have experienced what you have to offer. At this point, however, your potential customer hasn't made their decision yet. To explain how this final stage works, let me go back to the two examples that I shared in the previous section. The person in the first example had arranged for a twenty-four-hour test drive of their favourite car. They absolutely loved it, but they just weren't ready to make the commitment. As the weeks go by, they continue to look at the car on social media, still in the consideration stage. If you remember, they were asked to explain what their ideal specification would have been from their favourite model. Armed with this information, the car dealer has a plan. The dream specification and model just happen to come into the showroom, so the dealer decides to send a photo of the car to the prospective customer. In the message, the dealer says that this car is the exact specification that they were looking for. In one second, the customer switched from consideration to conversion; that message and photo was all they needed to see. Within a week, they were down at the showroom signing the documents and driving away in their dream car. This process might have taken a little while, but it worked perfectly. This was a well-executed marketing conveyor belt (or funnel).

Now let's have a look at the personal training example. Your potential customer had a holiday booked in four months and they were struggling with their diet. At the end of the fourteen days, they weren't ready to invest. Over the next four weeks, you keep speaking to them and giving them even more tips. They lost a further 5 lbs under your free guidance. During this time, you'd saved their email address, and you had added them to your weekly client email list. Every Friday, you send out a friendly email to your current and potential clients. One week in particular, you write about holiday dieting and time frames to achieve goals, and you also share a set of before-and-after pictures of one of your clients who was due to go on holiday. Knowing how much you wanted to work with the client who had lost 15 lbs for free, you chose a transformation that was very similar to what theirs could be. Within a few hours of sending out the email, they reply asking you if it's possible to start coaching with you. All they needed at this stage was to see someone who had achieved similar results. Your persistence and understanding of marketing paid off. You'd seen the process all the way through from awareness, to consideration, to conversion.

A conversion requires something that convinces your potential customer to invest in you, your products or your services.

Here are some strategies to consider:

- Provide a specific discount or promotion price
- Highlight the uniqueness of your product or service – the key points of differentiation that your audience can't get anywhere else

- Highlight the deep emotional reasons why your audience are considering your product or service

- Provide a limited time frame that your audience has for purchasing, creating a high level of urgency

- Showcase client results that your audience can relate to

- Showcase happy customers that your audience can relate to

So that you fully appreciate this stage, think back to the last purchase you made. What was it that tipped you over the edge? What did the company do, say or show you that made you turn your consideration into an investment?

The conversion stage is vital in the marketing process; without it you won't have any new customers. Right now, it's likely that you're missing out on working with a lot of people simply because you're not using the strategies above to push your audience over the edge.

PIT STOP

Do you now see the role that the marketing journey and relationship building plays in your ability to work with more people? If you can't reach them, you'll never stand a chance of working with them. As a fitness professional, it's important for you to get better at this. It does takes time, so be patient, keep track of what you're doing, assess it at all times, and continue to refine your systems.

At the start of the marketing section, I said that there are two additional stages that play a large role in supporting the development of your reputation, your ability to achieve results with your clients and the growth of your business. In my opinion, your reputation is one of your greatest marketing tools. If you build it well, your clients should do a large percentage of your marketing for you. However, to get people to talk about you they need to experience enough of you, your product or service. For that to happen, you need to keep them engaged with your business.

Retention

When it comes to retention, there are two main areas to consider: keeping hold of individual clients from a personal training, online-training or small-group perspective; and keeping hold of a member so that you have a better opportunity to introduce them to more products and services. For gyms and studios, member retention also plays an essential role in the overall financial development of the business.

How does retention play its role in marketing for personal trainers, online trainers and group coaching? The majority of trainers don't think about the long game – they think session to session, month to month, or block to block. This goes back to the difference between a fitness professional and a fitness business professional. Whenever I would start a coaching relationship with a new client, I immediately looked at it from a professional perspective. If I did everything in my power, what could my client achieve? If I could help them to go far beyond what they can see at this moment, would their results help me to develop my reputation? With an improved reputation, I could reach more people, I could get even more results and I could eventually charge more. For this to happen, I had to go into each session with retention in my mind. My client might be thinking about the twelve-week block of training that they'd paid for, but I needed them to be with me for at least six months.

Every single client is a ticket to the next level of your career. If you truly want to Level Up at every opportunity, you have to make client retention a top priority. I speak to many trainers who say that their clients just came to the end of their package and stopped coaching, or they seemed to lose motivation and cancelled the remainder of their sessions. In a lot of cases, these are both classic examples of training someone instead of coaching them – focusing session to session, without having a longer-term vision and a result-focused road map in place. If, however, your clients do genuinely come to the end of a set period of time working with you, this isn't the time to let your relationship with them slide. Keeping in touch still influences retention because there is always a strong chance that they'll come back further down the line. So, make sure you don't see your past clients as finished; they still need marketing to.

One of the main reasons why our results are so consistent at M10 is because the average length of time that our clients are with us is six months. We take our retention strategies seriously because a client who stays with you and continues to make progress will always be one of your best marketing assets.

Here are some key areas to focus on when it comes to client retention:

- Provide a detailed road map for your clients to follow; go beyond workouts and training plans. If your clients see a step-by-step road map, they have something to focus on and buy into.

- Focus on delivering a high-quality customer experience (refer back to the 'Branding' section).

- Ask your clients for feedback regularly. This shows your commitment to keep delivering a high level of service.

- Commit to your education and use this to educate your clients. The more your clients learn, the more they'll be invested in the coaching process.

- Make each client feel valued when you're coaching them. Listen to them and always be attentive.

- Maintain regular communication each week (even when your client isn't working with you).

- Acknowledge and reward all of your client's successes and milestones throughout their journey. Each level of success increases your perceived value to them as their coach.

- Provide your clients with additional resources that they can refer to throughout the coaching process.

When it comes to members of a gym/studio, retention plays a huge part in your marketing strategies. If all of your marketing efforts go into looking for new customers, you'll forget to look after the ones that you already have. While many will see this as part of the operations and customer service part of a business, I like to include it in marketing as well. Keeping customers engaged and building relationships with them is very much about marketing. So many businesses struggle to grow because existing members are leaving as fast as new members are joining. If members do leave, however, few businesses have follow-up marketing processes which focus on maintaining relationships. People do often leave, but that doesn't mean they won't come back.

Member retention is also key for revenue opportunities. The longer a member stays with you, the more likely they'll be to invest in products and services that you have for sale at your gym/studio. This is looking into the lifetime value of a customer. If you're on top of your retention strategies, one individual member will spend a lot more across the lifecycle of their membership.

Here are some key areas to focus on when it comes to member retention:

- Ask for regular member feedback – this shows your commitment to continue delivering a high-quality service

- Create member loyalty programmes

- Send regular member emails offering free advice and education

- Keep in touch with former members through platforms such as email and social media

- Create member events

The big take-home for you regarding retention is that it is part of your marketing road map. Focusing solely on acquiring new customers will be useless to you if you lose them after a couple of months. Make sure you look after your customers and keep them in your business; they'll achieve better results, your business will be a lot more stable, and they'll help you by doing a lot of your marketing for you.

Referral

Happy clients tell their friends; this is one of your most valuable marketing strategies. Can you imagine where your business would be right now if each of your clients referred someone to you? Referrals aren't just an opportunity to meet a prospective new client; they are a sign that you are doing a good job. Your clients are so happy with the level of service that you're providing for them that they feel compelled to tell their friends, family members or colleagues.

I am a firm believer that referrals are earned. Over the years, I've been advised by quite a few mentors to ask for referrals, but that strategy has never yielded me a valuable client. Often, you ask your client if they know anyone that they think would benefit from working with you. They share the details of one or two friends, and you give them a call. They might have heard their friend mention you, but they haven't directly asked to be referred to you. You feel like you're explaining yourself on the call, and they're not showing a lot of interest. This isn't a referral that's been earned, and as such I wouldn't place this strategy at the top of my marketing list.

I see referrals as a marketing strategy for the very reason that you can create them. Coaches often just expect their clients to tell their friends, family members or colleagues about them, but this isn't how it works. There are plenty of things that you can do to ensure that your clients tell people about you.

Think back to the last time that you told a friend to go to a restaurant that you'd recently been to. Was it a run-of-the-mill restaurant with mediocre service? Or was there something that you experienced that made you want to message all your friends to tell them about it? Restaurants know what they want people to say about their businesses, which is why they focus on referral marketing strategies. They know what their clientele sees as a valuable experience, so a good restaurant will double down on providing it. As a result, time and time again, people come in for the first time off the back of a referral from a friend or family member.

PIT STOP

Do you know what your clients' expectations are? Do you know what they perceive as high value?

Your clients may have told you what their goals are, but there's a lot more that you want them to tell their friends. Refer back to the 'Branding' section, where I asked you to review your customer experience. People love high-quality service, and they love feeling valued. Are you going above and beyond to meet your clients' expectations? You might be pushing so hard to help them to lose weight that you lose sight of the customer experience. If so, you're missing out on the opportunity for them to go home and tell their partner how amazing your level of service is. If you think that your client values your training the most, when in fact they value education a lot more, you're missing out on the opportunity for them to tell their friends how much they're learning from working with you. A referral doesn't have to mean that someone hands their friend's phone number to you; it could simply mean that your clients feel so strongly about their experience with you that they regularly bring it up in conversation with their friends, family members or colleagues. If you become a talking point, you are doing a good job with your referral marketing and it's only a matter of time before your contact details start being handed around.

There will also be times when your clients talk about their friends, family members or colleagues, and they say that they should be doing a bit more for their health and fitness. At this stage, I wouldn't ask for a referral, but you can influence the conversations that they have. You can share tips and pieces of advice, or you can tell them to get their friends to start following you on social media. You could even get their friends to join your mailing list so that they can start learning from you. While this isn't a direct referral, it's the start of the conveyor belt. If you keep listening when you talk to your clients, there is often someone that they know who you can start to work on.

It goes without saying that results play a key role in receiving referrals. When your clients start to change shape or get close to achieving their goals, it's often not long before friends, family members or colleagues start asking for your contact details. If results aren't coming in thick and fast for you, make sure you're focusing on getting referrals for your professionalism, knowledge, customer service and attention to detail. I know that if you apply everything that I have covered in this book, your referrals will increase. The simple act of becoming a lot more professional will be noticed by your clients.

The final thing that I'll say about referrals is that they are the secret to being able to increase your prices. A referral is coming to you because someone has told them to contact you. This is a lot more valuable than speaking to someone who doesn't know you at all. The person who has been referred to you will also perceive you to have a higher value. I'm not saying that you should increase your fees for every referral, but when you're ready to increase your hourly/monthly rate, one of the first places I'd start with is referrals. A lot of fitness professionals struggle to increase their prices for fear of losing clients, but when you start to charge more to referral clients, how you value yourself will completely change. When I was charging £40 per hour, I started to receive quite a few referrals. It had been a year since I pushed my prices up, so I decided to put my next referral at £50 per hour. It was daunting at the time, but I valued myself, so I went with it. Over the next few weeks, I took on a few more clients at £50 per hour. I had eight of my weekly sessions now being charged at £50. As soon as I saw that, I didn't have any fear of putting my £40 clients up by £5 per hour. The value that I had for myself had shot up. I did the same six to eight months later, while still taking more new clients on at £50 per hour. This was a strategy that I scaled up to over £85 per hour, and it was all off the back of referrals.

There are many more layers to marketing, such as copywriting, local marketing, email marketing, social media, websites and paid advertising. I don't want this to be the end of your marketing journey, as there is so much more for you to learn and so much more that you and your business can benefit from. Without learning what I've taught you in this section first, though, you would be using individual strategies without any clear customer journey. People would land on your website and be unclear on what to do. They'd see your content and they wouldn't understand who it's aimed at. Now that you understand the marketing conveyor belt, you'll have a new appreciation for the journey that your potential customers need to go on.

Sales

What kind of relationship do you have with sales and money? If you're like a lot of the fitness professionals that I speak to, it's not great. As a result, it's likely that you're not seeing your financial growth increasing in line with your expectation. Most of you will think that sales is a sleazy subject, that it's pushy and not the reason that you got into the fitness industry. If I'm honest, in the early days I felt exactly the same.

I would struggle to ask for money if I knew a client was behind with their payments, and I would always cringe at the end of a consultation when it was time to present the pricing for my coaching packages. I didn't know it at the time, but I was struggling with my perception of sales and money. I didn't want people to see me as someone who was purely focused on making money; I wanted people to know me for my level of professionalism and for the quality of my results. So, rather than valuing sales, I did my best to avoid it.

As part of our training when I worked as a personal trainer at LA Fitness, there was one day when we covered sales. We went through the consultation process and how to present our coaching packages, and we learned some basic closing strategies. This was the first time that I realised that there was a process to sales, and it was when the penny dropped for me. I realised that if I could nail down the sales process, I could not only train more clients, but I could sign them up for more sessions each week. More clients and more sessions equal more results, which will have a positive impact on my reputation as well as allow me to help more people. I was also able to link sales to being able to afford more education, which meant that my clients would learn more, and in turn they'd achieve their goals a lot quicker. Sales wasn't just helping me to get what I wanted; it was going to be helping my clients to get what they wanted, too. It dawned on me that there are so many people who are missing out on achieving their goals simply because they weren't being sold to.

Now if you're still struggling a bit with the word 'sales', let me help you to look at it from a slightly different angle. I once had the whole process explained to me as 'helping someone to come to a decision'. Every day, you see people who know that they want to make a change, but they have so many different things running through their minds. In fact, they know that they want to invest in themselves, they just don't know the best route to take. The whole sales process is only going to benefit them, as it ties together everything that they're confused about and helps them to come to a clear and concise decision.

At this point, my whole perception of sales had changed. I no longer saw it as something bad. I had a responsibility to sell; I had a responsibility to help people achieve their goals. I had also made a commitment to myself that I would develop my reputation, that I would be known for my craft, and there was no way that was going to happen if I didn't Level Up with my sales process.

For your business to grow, and for you to reach your goals, you have to learn to not only value sales but to enjoy it. I hope your perception of sales has changed after reading this section. For your business to progress, you do have to overcome any limitations around sales; it has to become one of your strengths.

Sales is a process; it only gets better the more you test and refine it. You have to have a script, something that you can follow step by step, to measure the effectiveness of each stage. If you follow a different strategy every time, you won't have anything to test.

You have to understand who you are talking to. This is crucial because sales start from the awareness stage of your marketing. Firstly, you focus on getting the attention of your target audience, then you use your marketing content or face-to-face conversations to deepen the relationship. It's only at the conversion stage that you're ready to move into the actual sale (where you get the commitment from your customer). Remember that people buy from people they like. But people also buy from people they trust. The longer you spend getting to know someone, the more trust they will have built in you. It's vital that your marketing talks to your audience in a language that they understand and can relate to. There's no point trying to sell your services or products to an audience that is confused. An audience that hasn't built trust is often an audience that will say no; so, prior to selling, always make sure that you're building relationships with your target audience and refining all of your marketing systems.

The whole sales process starts with an enquiry. Someone shows a committed level of interest in your products or services. This is not a sale – far from it; this is when the work begins. For someone to make a genuine enquiry, it's likely that there has been something that has tipped them over the edge. Maybe they saw a testimonial that you posted on your social media, maybe they read an article which related to the same problems that they were facing, or maybe they saw you working with someone in the gym whom they could relate to. Whatever it was, they've made contact with you, and they want to know more. Now, in a lot of cases you panic, you tell them about your coaching services or your membership options, and then you tell them the price. This is the quickest way to end up with a 'no'. All of the hard work that you've put into your marketing to get them to this point has been for nothing. It's easy to lose a sale, and it's often because you think that people have enquired to learn more about you and your services. This couldn't be further from the truth; they've made their enquiry because there is something that they want or need. They might have asked you to tell them more about what you do, but you need to turn this back around to them.

There is selling where you are sat down with someone face to face, there is selling on the phone, and then there is sales copywriting. I'm going to give you an overview of the first two in this section. Sales copywriting involves writing text (copy) with the intention of acquiring a sale at the end. I'm sure you've read pages on websites or inside magazines, where the content has flowed in such a way that you feel compelled to purchase the product at the end. This is used mostly when the customer isn't going to have direct contact with the seller. Sales copywriting is a learned skill, so if you have products and services that you sell online, I would urge you to start studying it. A lot of what I have learned about face-to-face selling has come from studying sales copywriting, because they do share similarities. They are both processes where the goal is to acquire a sale at the end, and they are both based around psychology.

Developing an emotional connection

The first stage when you speak to someone is to understand their why. What do they want to achieve, and why is it so important to them? As I said in the introduction to the Sales section, they might want to know what you do and how much you charge, but this isn't why they've contacted you. It often takes a little time to find out someone's motivation to change, but you must be persistent. Their reason becomes their anchor, which is the thing that you can get them to relate back to at any stage throughout the coaching process. Think of a father who makes an enquiry with you. At first, he says he wants to lose weight, but before you take him any further, you tell him that it depends on his specific goals and realistic time frames. This immediately turns it back on him. After some deep questioning, he reveals that he's sick and tired of looking in the mirror and not liking how he looks. He's got a two-year-old and doesn't want to be the out-of-shape dad when his baby grows up. This is where emotion comes in because for a sale to happen, there has to be emotion. Getting the father to open up has revealed his why. This is going to be his reason for making the investment at the end of the sales process. But here's the thing to always remember: nothing about this process is forcing him to buy. He's identified that this is a big deal for him, so all you're about to do is help him to come to the decision that your coaching is what he needs.

Visualise the end goal

After you've established an emotional connection, the next stage is to try to get your client to start imagining that they have achieved their goal. This is a valuable step, and one that is often missed out. A simple question that you could ask is, 'Can you explain how it would feel to have achieved your goal?' As soon as they do, their perceived value of your coaching will increase. A main priority as we're going through each stage is raising the perceived value your clients have of you. At the start, they're focused on price; now you're making them focus so much more on their goal and how it will make them feel.

How are you going to get there?

Now that they know how important their goal is to them, and they can clearly picture themselves achieving it, there is the part in between – how they're going to get there. A question I always ask at this stage is, 'What do you think you need to know more about in order to reach your goals?' In the case of a fat-loss goal, often the person that you're speaking to will say that they don't know enough about nutrition, or that they have no clue where to start when it comes to creating a training programme. Better still, they'll tell you that they don't know how to push themselves in the gym or how to stay motivated. It's important for your prospect to tell you what they don't know and the areas where they're struggling, because this is them admitting that they can't achieve their goals on their own. Again, this is just increasing their perceived value of you as you go through the process.

Education and credibility

Once they have highlighted what they don't know, and clearly identified that they need help, this is your opportunity to explain a little bit more about the areas that they've highlighted. You could talk through a case study of a client who had similar goals; you could start to inform them in the areas that they know little about; or, better still, you could show your prospect some results from clients that you have worked with. Hopefully they will have engaged with your content or seen your results through your marketing, but it's important that you give them a reminder.

Review

At this point, your prospect has highlighted how important their goal is to them, they've visualised themselves achieving their goal, and they've acknowledged that they don't know enough. If this was you being walked through the sales process, what would you be thinking now? I hope you'd be thinking that you need to progress and sign up. It's easy to jump stages if you think that your prospect is showing signs that they're ready to invest, but you need to follow the process until you're fully proficient at it. At this stage, the best thing you can do is take your time to provide your prospect with a full review. Go back over their goal and get them to agree that it's definitely what they want to achieve. Paint the picture of them achieving their goal and remind them how they will feel. Get them to confirm to you again that it's exactly where they want to get to. Then, go back over the areas that they don't know enough about and ask them, 'If I were able to teach you everything that you don't know and create a structured plan for you to follow, do you think you'd reach your goal?' This is a crucial part of the sales process because you're looking for that all-important confirmation.

Presentation

If your prospect says 'yes' (which they should), the next stage is to present the full coaching journey for them, with the pricing package. Make sure you explain each stage that you're going to take them through before providing them with the price. This is an important point, because once you give the price, you're going to pause. You have to be strong enough to not say anything until they speak next. I learned this way back when I attended the LA Fitness sales training. You will often feel the need to justify your pricing, and you end up going off on a tangent. Remember, you have taken your prospect through a complete process; there's nothing else you need to say. Just wait for them to speak first. Hopefully your prospect says 'yes', and you have yourself a new client.

Uncertainty

If they seem unsure, like they can't make up their mind, it's likely that you've missed a part of the process or you haven't answered some of their questions. My advice to you here is to think back through each stage. Go back through everything with them, remind of everything that you've said, and make them aware of everything that they agreed with. A quick recap, answering some extra questions, or adding in the section that you missed is often enough for you to pull it back round. Don't give up when someone tries to pull back; they likely just need a little more reassurance.

Objections

There will often be objections when you're going through a sales process. I simply see them as barriers.

You just need to work out what could be holding your prospect back and then you need to connect the dots. One of the best ways that I handle objections is I bring them up as I'm going through the sales process. If you know someone is going to use limited time as an objection, cover the range of hours that you're available. If you think they're going to bring up meal preparation and how long it takes, bring up how you teach making quick and easy meals, and – even better still – you have a meal prep company who can bring meals to their work. Over time, you will build up a list of objections that you'll be able to counter with each type of prospect. Answering objections before your prospect has the chance to raise them will not only increase the perceived value of your coaching service, it gives them no other option but to sign up.

Objections is a lengthy subject, and one that I suggest that you do some more research into. If you're constantly faced with objections, I would suggest you review your full marketing systems and your sales process. The better you get at both, the easier each sale will get.

It's also important to understand that the word 'no' is part of sales. You need to hear 'no' to have something to learn from. I always go into every sales consultation with the belief that I'm going to close the sale, but my head doesn't go down if it doesn't happen. There will always have been something that I could have done differently, and it could go right back to the start of the marketing journey. When someone says 'no', it's also important to remember that your prospect isn't saying 'no' to you personally; they're saying 'no' to your sales consultation process and your product/ service. Don't take it to heart; you just need to work on your presentation.

Sales is a fascinating field, and I have spent a lot of time studying and refining my thinking around it. When you create your content, speak to people, write articles or even speak at events, sales should always be at the forefront of your mind. You might not be planning on selling at that moment in time, but every interaction plays its part in the marketing journey and will lead you closer to the start of the sales process.

When you use the steps that I have shared in this section, make sure that you put your own personality into them, and make sure that you practice them. Before every sales consultation, I sit down for at least twenty minutes and prepare myself. Where so many coaches fall down is they jump into a sales consultation and wing it. If you want to build your reputation, increase your client results and ultimately earn more income, make sure you take each sales consultation seriously.

360 degrees of excellence to Do More!

Take time right now to do a 360 degrees of excellence check in. Ask yourself:

1. Am I growing as a person?

2. Am I developing a better reputation?

3. Are my results where I want them to be?

4. Is my business growing?

If you haven't done so yet, write out these check-in questions where you can see them every day. If you're committed to progress, you'll use them regularly to hold yourself accountable.

A fitness business professional has their goals in mind when they operate each day and they are target focused. They are a lot more disciplined with planning and time management, and they are less likely to be distracted because they are so focused on achieving their goals and vision. Discipline is crucial in order to be able fulfil the many roles that form part of the Professional road map – and in order to be able to wear the many professional hats required. Fitness business professionals are disciplined with their money, marketing themselves and so their brand, customer service and in understanding how all these facets impact the growth of their business and progress through life. I hope you have learned some of the key elements of growing your business and developing a business mindset in the Professional part of *Level Up*.

Final Thoughts

I hardly read anything at school; the only book that I remember sitting down and reading from start to finish was *Danny the Champion of the World* by Roald Dahl. For so many years I struggled to connect the dots between reading, education and the impact it can have on your life, so to be sitting here writing the final section of my own book blows my mind. It also fills me with immense pride and gratitude.

I know you want to achieve something with your life and with your business. For some of you, that might seem a long way off right now. But I can promise you that if you do everything in your power to Level Up at every opportunity, you will keep progressing. I've never worried about time; I knew I had plenty of it. I've always been more concerned with how I spend it. Make sure you can see your vision clearly, and never forget that your destination is the sum of the action that you're prepared to take: *we all have the same amount of time throughout our careers, it's what you do with it that counts.*

Confidence is the result of taking consistent action; this is something that I have learned throughout my career. I didn't have a lot of it when I was younger, but it's grown immensely year on year. Just like time, I never focused on it; I always knew it was the by-product of hard work and results. Many of you will be searching for confidence, but it's something that you receive when you make progress and when you commit to levelling up. You can't expect to become more confident if you stay the same.

I've covered many topics in *Level Up*, and as an avid reader myself, I know how easy it is to get so focused on one part that you forget some of the earlier sections. But I want you to take as much as you can from each section. I wrote *Level Up* for people with all levels of experience in the fitness industry. Every section has something that you can take away. If you're new to the industry, you now have a full road map to follow for your entire career. If you're a lot more experienced, it's likely that there will be a few sections that you're have already familiar with. However, you might have skipped them and not seen them as important at the time. You might now be ready to reach a wider audience and increase your income, in which case you'll take a lot away from the marketing and finance section. But here is why the whole book will be important to you: No matter what level you're at right now, you'll need to Level Up across each section if you want to see consistent progress. If you want to earn more, you will need to address your vision (Personal). You'll need to increase your education and reputation (Physical), and you'll need to develop new products/ services and improve your marketing (Professional). If you're new to the industry and you want to fill your personal training diary, it's essential that you learn and address any personal limitations or perceptions of low self-confidence (Personal). You will need to choose the most appropriate education for your current fitness level, and you'll need to start applying what you know to yourself (Physical). You'll also need to learn the foundations of business (Professional).

Every time I want to push forward in any area of my life or business, I use the Level Up road map. There is always something in each section that I need to work on that will propel me to the next level. The greatest athletes and businesspeople are incredibly disciplined and they're constantly looking for ways to improve. They analyse all aspects of their lives, looking for that extra 5% where they can grow. You have to develop this mindset if you want to excel. This is why we should study those who have achieved great levels of success – because their achievements give us the greatest insight into what it takes.

Excellence has no finish line. If you want to have the best life and you want to be truly happy and fulfilled, you must commit to never-ending progress. Take what you can from *Level Up* right now, and make sure you keep coming back to it. As you go through, make notes, colour in certain sections, do whatever you need to, to make sure that it becomes a valuable tool as you progress through your career.

I want my legacy to be all about possibility. I want to help as many of you as I can to achieve something that you never thought was possible. As a coach, I always had this in my mind for my clients. It's incredibly rewarding whenever someone tells me that they never thought they'd ever look the way that they do. Now I am in a position to use my own career and the lessons that I've learned to give back to you – to ensure that you get the opportunity to change people's lives and show them that they can achieve anything. I want you to make your own impact on the fitness industry and achieve your own level of success, fulfilment and happiness.

Thank you for coming on this Level Up journey with me. From the bottom of my heart, I am eternally grateful that you have invested in me, and I hope that I have been a support to you, your life and your career.

Further Reading

Personal – Be More

Burchard, B, *High Performance Habits: How extraordinary people become that way* (Hay House Inc, 2017)

Byrne, R, *The Magic* (Simon & Schuster Ltd, 2012)

Carnegie, D, *How To Win Friends And Influence People* (Vermilion, 2006)

Demartini, JF, *The Values Factor: The secret to creating an inspired and fulfilling life* (Berkley Books, 2013)

Grover, T, *Relentless: From good to great to unstoppable* (Atria Books, 2014)

Heath, D & C, *Switch: How to change things when change is hard* (Random House Business, 2011)

Keller, G, *The One Thing: The surprisingly simple truth behind extraordinary results* (John Murray Learning, 2014)

Peters, Dr S, *The Chimp Paradox: The mind management programme for confidence, success, and happiness* (Vermilion, 2012)

Peters, Dr S, *The Silent: Understanding and developing the mind throughout life* (Lagom, 2018)

Peterson, JB, *12 Rules For Life: An antidote to chaos* (Penguin, 2018)

Rath, T, *Strengthsfinder 2.0: Discover your CliftonStrengths* (Gallup Press, 2007)

Robbins, T, *Awaken The Giant Within: How to take immediate control of your mental, emotional, physical and financial life* (Simon & Schuster UK, 2001)

Robbins, T, *Unlimited Power: The new science of personal achievement* (Simon & Schuster UK, 2001)

Rotella, Dr B, *How Champions Think: In sport and in life* (Simon & Schuster, 2016)

Sharma, R, *The Monk Who Sold His Ferrari* (Harper Thorson, 2015)

Sharma, R, *The 5AM Club* (Harper Thorsons, 2018)

Sinek, S, *Start With Why: How great leaders inspire everyone to take action* (Penguin, 2011)

Sinek, S, *Find Your Why: A practical guide for discovering purpose for you or your team* (Portfolio Penguin, 2017)

Physical - Learn More

Bompa, T and Buzzichelli, C, *Periodization Training For Sports* (Human Kinetics, 2015)

Boyle, M, *Advances In Functional Training* (On Target Publications, 2011)

Clark, N, *Nancy Clark's Sports Nutrition Guidebook* (Human Kinetics, 2013)

Cook, G, *Movement: Functional movement systems: screening, assessment, corrective strategies* (On Target Publications, 2011)

Gambetta, V, *Athletic development: The art and science of functional sports conditioning* (Human Kinetics, 2006)

Hinson, J, Raven, P & Shern, L, *The Endocrine System: Systems of the body* (Churchill Livingstone, 2010)

Hofmekler, O, *Maximum Muscle Minimum Fat: The secret science behind physical transformation* (North Atlantic Books, 2008)

Holford, P, *The Optimum Nutrition Bible* (Piatkus, 1997)

Holford, P and Neil, K, *Balance Your Hormones: The simple drug-free way to solve women's health problems* (Piatkus, 2011)

Hyman, M, *The UltraSimple Diet: Kick-start your metabolism and safely lose up to 10 pounds in 7 days* (Pocket Books, 2008)

Hyman, M, *Ultra Mind Solution: The simple way to defeat depression, overcome anxiety, and sharpen your mind* (Scribner, 2010)

Hyman, M, *The Blood Sugar Solution 10-Day Detox Diet: The bestselling programme for preventing diabetes, losing weight and feeling great* (Hodder & Stoughton, 2012)

Kraemer, W, and Fleck, S, *Designing Resistance Training Programs* (Human Kinetics Publishers, 3rd edn, 2003)

Levangie, P & Norkin C, *Joint Structure And Function: A comprehensive analysis* (2011)

Lee, Dr J, *What Your Doctor May Not Tell You About Premenopause* (Grand Central Publishing, 2000)

Lee, Dr J & Hopkins, V, *What Your Doctor May Not Tell You About The Menopause* (Life and Style, 2005)

Lee, Dr J & Hopkins, V, *Hormone Balance Made Simple* (Life and Style, 2006)

McGill, S, *Back Mechanics* (Backfitpro Inc, 2015)

McGill, S, *Lower Back Disorders* (Human Kinectics, 2016)

Pasquale, M, *The Metabolic Diet* (AllProTraining.com Books, 2000)

Rothfeld, G and Romaine, D, *Thyroid Balance: Traditional and alternative methods for treating thyroid disorders* (Adams Media, 2002)

Sapolsky, R, *Why Zebras Get Ulcers* (St Martin's Press, 2004)

Schoenfeld, B, *Science And Development Of Muscle Hypertrophy* (Human Kinetics, 2016)

Stone, J & R, *Atlas Of Skeletal Muscles* (McGraw-Hill Education, 2011)

Verkhoshansky, Y & N, *Special Strength Training: Manual for coaches* (Verkhoshansky.com, 2011)

Professional – Do More

Bly, R, *The Copywriter's Handbook: A step-by-step guide to writing copy that sells* (Owl Books, 2006)

Brunson, R, *Dotcom Secrets: The underground playbook for growing your company online* (Morgan James Publishing, 2015)

Brunson, R, *Expert Secrets: The underground playbook for creating a mass movement of people who will pay for your advice* (Morgan James Publishing, 2017)

Cialdini, R, *Influence: The psychology of persuasion* (William Morrow, 1999)

Covey, S, *The 7 Habits Of Highly Effective People* (Running Press, 2000)

Denny, R, *Selling To Win* (Kogan Page, 2013)

Gallo, C, *The Storyteller's Secret: How TED speakers and inspirational leaders turn their passion into performance* (Macmillan, 2018)

Gerber, M, *The E-myth Revisited: Why most small businesses don't work and what to do about it* (Harper Business, 2001)

Gitomer, J, *Sales Bible: The ultimate sales resource* (John Wiley & Sons Inc, 2015)

Godin, S, *Permission Marketing: Strangers into friends into customers* (Simon & Schuster, 2007)

Kennedy, D, *Speak to Sell: Persuade, influence, and establish authority & promote your products, services, practice, business, or cause* (Advantage Media Group, 2016)

Knight, P, *Shoe Dog: A memoir by the creator of NIKE* (Simon & Schuster, 2018)

Maslen, A, *Write to Sell: The ultimate guide to copywriting* (Marshall Cavendish International, 2019)

McKee, R, *Storynomics: Story-driven marketing in the post-advertising world* (Hachette, 2018)

McKeown, G, *Essentialism: The disciplined pursuit of less* (Crown Business, 2014)

Port, M, *Book Yourself Solid: The fastest, easiest, and most reliable system for getting more clients than you can handle even if you hate marketing and selling* (John Wiley & Sons, 2006)

Priestley, D, *Oversubscribed: How to get people lining up to do business with you* (Capstone, 2015)

Robbins, T, *Money Master The Game: 7 simple steps to financial freedom* (Simon & Schuster, 2014)

Schroeder, B, *Brands and Bullsh*t: Excel at the former and avoid the latter. a branding primer for millennial marketers in a digital age* (CreateSpace Independent Publishing Platform, 2017)

Syed, M, *Bounce: The myth of talent and the power of practice* (HarperCollins, 2011)

Syed, M, *Black Box Thinking: Marginal gains and the secrets of high performance* (John Murray, 2016)

Vaynerchuk, G, *Jab, Jab, Jab, Right Hook: How to Tell Your Story in a Noisy, Social World* (Harpur Business, 2013)

Whitman, D, *Cashvertising: How to use more than 100 secrets of ad-agency psychology to make big money selling anything to anyone* (Career Press, 2008)

Wickman, G and Winters, M, *Rocket Fuel: The one essential combination that will get you more of what you want from your business* (BenBella Books, 2016)

For more reading recommendations, visit M10life.com/resources

The Author

 Mark started in the fitness industry just like many coaches starting their career – in a health club. After building a successful personal training business and working his way up the management ladder, he decided it was time to go it alone. He opened his first M10 studio in 2006 and grew it to a team of five personal trainers. Once at capacity, he knew it was time for bigger and better, so in 2012 he opened his flagship M10 gym in Nottingham city centre. M10 has a team of seven personal trainers and a gym membership of 150 members. M10 is a centre of excellence for personal training.

Until 2015, Mark was a fully booked personal trainer and online coach, working with clients all over the world. He created multiple online fat-loss and muscle-building programmes, which enabled him to help even more people. While he was developing his brand and reputation, Mark was also a competitive bodybuilder and competed with the UK Bodybuilding Fitness Federation (UKBFF).

In 2010, he started to support fitness professionals with their careers and began offering private internships. In 2015, he extended this further and started M10 Education, with the goal of helping more personal trainers and fitness professionals across the globe. Mark and his team run courses and seminars throughout Europe, an in-house personal training mentorship, a business mastermind, 121 mentoring and multiple online fitness business courses.

Throughout his career, Mark's work has been published across world-leading press including *Flex* magazine, *Men's Health*, *Muscle & Fitness*, and *GQ* magazine. He is also a speaker, and he regularly presents at large events on the subjects of coaching and fitness business.

Mark has always had the attitude of improvement and constant progression, which is why his career has been constantly evolving. His mission is to give every fitness professional the opportunity to create their own fulfilling, successful and happy career.

After reading *Level Up*, many of you will be asking how you can learn from me and my team. You can find a list of our education programmes through our website at www.M10life.com/shop.

If you want to keep in touch and follow me as I keep on levelling up, contact me via:

◎ @markcolesm10

🅵 Mark Coles Coach

♫ Mastery podcast

✉ info@m10fitness.co.uk

⊕ www.m10fitness.co.uk & www.m10life.com

CPSIA information can be obtained
at www.ICGtesting.com
Printed in the USA
LVHW080852210720
661156LV00022B/888